true ghosts

2

About the Author

David Godwin (Lakeville, MN) is the managing editor of FATE magazine. He holds a Bachelor of Journalism degree from the University of Texas at Austin and is a student of esoteric lore, magic, and the Cabala.

To Write to the Author

If you wish to contact the author or would like more information about this book, please write to the author in care of Llewellyn Worldwide Ltd. and we will forward your request. Both the author and publisher appreciate hearing from you and learning of your enjoyment of this book and how it has helped you. Llewellyn Worldwide Ltd. cannot guarantee that every letter written to the author can be answered, but all will be forwarded. Please write to:

David Godwin
℅ Llewellyn Worldwide
2143 Wooddale Drive
Woodbury, MN 55125-2989

Please enclose a self-addressed stamped envelope for reply, or $1.00 to cover costs. If outside the U.S.A., enclose an international postal reply coupon.

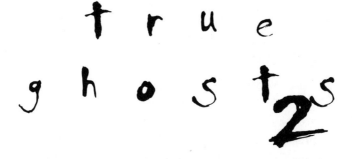

true ghosts 2

more haunting tales from the vaults of FATE magazine

unearthed and edited by
DAVID GODWIN

Llewellyn Publications
Woodbury, Minnesota

First Edition
First Printing, 2010

Based on book design by Steffani Sawyer
Cover art © iStockphoto.com/miljko
Cover design by Ellen Dahl
Editing by Ed Day
Llewellyn is a registered trademark of Llewellyn Worldwide Ltd.

Library of Congress Cataloging-in-Publication Data
True ghosts 2 : more haunting tales from the vaults of FATE magazine / unearthed and edited by David Godwin.—1st ed.
    p. cm.
  ISBN 978-0-7387-2294-8
  1. Ghosts. I. Godwin, David.
  BF1461.T78 2010
  133.1—dc22
                                        2010024215

Llewellyn Publications
A Division of Llewellyn Worldwide Ltd.
2143 Wooddale Drive
Woodbury, MN 55125-2989
www.llewellyn.com

Printed in the United States of America

Other books by David Godwin

*Light in Extension: Greek Magic from Homer to
Modern Times*

*Godwin's Cabalistic Encyclopedia: Complete
Guidance to Both Practical and Esoteric Applications*

Contents

Introduction

Do you need to *see* something to *believe* it? Ever see something, well, unbelievable? Good to hear. You are not alone.

We have all heard stories of family members or friends reaching out from beyond the grave, tales of ghosts and monsters, and rumors of premonitions, visions, out-of-body excursions, and astral walkabouts. But what can we really believe and where can we turn when seeking passage to the "other side"—the ferryman with his bony wrists and black cloak? Close, but not quite. Seek the experts at FATE magazine—ferrying people to tales from FATE beyond the threshold for over six decades and counting.

FATE magazine has continuously documented cases of the paranormal and unknown since 1948, making it the longest-standing publication of its kind. Breaking the Amityville Horror and the Roswell incident, FATE has been at the forefront of paranormal discovery and exploration within modern memory. Engaging its global audience actively, FATE has always given its readers a chance to submit experiences of the strange and unknown. As a result, the magazine possesses a unique amalgamation of the unidentified—hundreds-of-thousands of accounts—complete with sworn affidavits from the authors themselves.

As the associate editor of FATE magazine, I have had the unique privilege of consolidating hundreds of these true ghost stories, leaving me to question what most of the world would deem "impossible." I have learned through this process that stepping outside of material definitions is crucial for understanding the spirit world, tending to remind myself that descriptions of our universe are in constant flux, with metaphysics peeling back dimensional layers today in ways we never thought possible just a decade ago.

Since as individuals we are lucky to experience even one true paranormal event in our lives, cataloguing and consolidating our experiences through an authoritative and coherent means becomes crucial for understanding the "bigger picture." That is our mission at FATE, to make sense of the murky beyond with rich, residual archives, giving truth-seekers an outlet for fleshing-out similarities between seemingly disparate accounts of the truly bizarre, and to explore the fringe science challenging our ever-changing conception of what is possible.

The results, one will find, are surprising and inspirational, tear-jerking and sidesplitting, and whimsical and brooding, reminding those who have lost loved ones at one time or another that the spirit does indeed survive the body.

Within the idiosyncrasies and affinities shared by these stories lie doorways to collective truths, where sworn eyewitness testimony and good old fashioned believing provide vantage points for reaching beyond mere entrenched motifs of life and death, providing hope that life does not summarize existence. Ultimately we hope that this book reaches the people that truly need it, reminding the weary that *you are not alone*, neither in your experiences nor in your beliefs.

We all have to make sense of this world in our own ways. Why not start at the one place we all ultimately end: Death? Wherever the "thereafter" may be, we will leave up to you, but maybe these accounts will test those beliefs.

Messages from the Dead

Communication between the dead and the living is nothing new to this plane. Nowhere has this trend been more pronounced than between the family and friends of the departed. But how can we be sure that these phenomena aren't mere coping mechanisms projected by the grieving mind to protect the psyche from a starker reality? Is there nowhere tangible to probe for the truth in this world of the living?

For starters, we can look to each other. According to a Gallup Poll taken in 2005, a surprising 32 percent of Americans said they believed in ghosts. That same year, CBS affirmed at least in part that seeing is believing, with 22 percent of respondents expressing having seen or felt a ghost before.

Not too shabby for a subject so often shelved away by skeptics alongside the Easter Bunny and Santa Claus. But where do people form these beliefs?

For most people, said convictions stem from personal encounters with the dead. Messages from the dead are received in many forms. Some are read through symbols and the manipulation of objects, while others may be heard or felt vividly by the loved ones of the deceased through lucid, unmistakable apparitions.

Though these messages vary in content, one trend seemingly transcends the spectrum: Commune with the dead is often transformative, positive, and life changing for the living, giving new hope and shining light on the bleak and fallowed fields of tragedy. Here is the cream of the crop—those gleaming beacons of light that FATE has collected over the years—that will hopefully shine some light on the truth.

What Are Yellow and Black Butterflies?

Monday, April 17, 2001, was a day I will never forget—not only because it was the day after Easter, but also because it was the worst day of my life.

I was working second shift at a job I hated, rapidly shucking jewelry from raggedy, cardboard gift boxes and checking them for defects. The music blaring overhead played tunes that did not appeal to me. The entire atmosphere was engulfed with the buzzing, clicking, and banging of machinery.

The only reason I had taken this crummy job was that I was new to Cincinnati. My beau and I had moved from Atlanta in March. I wanted to explore a bit, and he was from Cincinnati. The one thing I regretted was leaving my mother behind.

My mother was truly more than a mother to me— she was also my best friend. My mother was an intelligent, eccentric woman, and very talented. She was free-spirited and big on self-statement. My brother and I were born and raised Wiccans. Imagine my awkwardness growing up black and Pagan when all my friends were Christians. Envision my frustration loving rock music when all my friends liked rap and R & B. But I wouldn't change for anything in the world!

I whiled away the ten-hour work night thinking about my mother—how much I missed her, and how I did not get to talk to her the day before. I mailed her a card, but I was quite certain she had not received it yet. Suddenly, "music to my ears" struck my soul like the thunder of Goddess: The song "Dog and Butterfly" by Heart began to play. My mother used to sing that song to me when I was a child. As the song played, I felt a peaceful, spiritual link to my mother, yet I was uncontrollably misty-eyed. I discreetly excused myself from my workstation and went to the bathroom. I closed my eyes and saw an enormous, yellow and black butterfly in my mind. Once I had composed myself, I went back to my work station and continued with my duties.

On the way home, I could not shake the image of the butterfly in my mind. My beau could tell I was upset. When he asked what was wrong, I replied, "I'm having the strangest feeling. I can't explain what it is or why. Something has happened . . ."

As we entered our apartment, I noticed the message light flashing on the answering machine. I ran over and listened to the message. It was from my great-uncle and brother, sadly stating, "NoShell, call us when you get in. It doesn't matter what time it is . . ." Needless to say, I called immediately, with the image of the butterfly still fluttering in my mind.

The news was horrible: My mother had passed away earlier that very day from a blood clot in her leg that moved up to her lung. I collided with the ground from grief. Not my mother! She was so young, only 46! There was so much we had not done together. I asked the cliché questions: Goddess, why? Our family is already so small. Why didn't you take me instead? Why my mother? Why now? Why are you so cruel?

That night, in between sleeplessness, I kept dreaming about a tree and a small stream in a thicket—and of course the yellow and black butterfly. I did not know why. My mother was a nature lover—not just because she was Pagan; she actually wanted to make a career of it. She went to college to be a forest ranger when she was younger. All my life, we could never go past the woods without venturing in, or go past a tree or wild flower without acknowledging its beauty. The dream was perhaps her ideal heaven; she was at peace.

My beau rented a car and rushed me to Atlanta that Tuesday afternoon. "Dog and Butterfly" was really stuck in my head now. A strange thing occurred. It snowed all the way from Cincinnati to Atlanta. In the middle of April? The song mentions snow . . .

When I arrived in Atlanta's radio range, the song was not only playing on my favorite classic rock station, but a recorded interview with the band was airing also. Was my mother trying to communicate with me? The yellow-and-black butterfly was once again burned in my mind.

My mother had made it clear to everyone that she wanted to be cremated after death. My great-uncle informed me that they had visited a friend's acreage in Loganville, Georgia. My mother enjoyed walking their nature trail. Even though she was in frail health, she walked the entire trail, stopping to rest several times. When they reached the end of the trail, a sparkling creek, she turned to my uncle and exclaimed, "You know how much I love this! When I die, I want to be cremated and sprinkled out here."

After I handled the final business, family and friends met with my brother and me to sprinkle my mother's ashes near the creek. We planted a seedling in the thicket and sprinkled her ashes there also. As the crowd dispersed back to the main house, my brother and I removed our necklaces—mine, a large, silver pentacle and his, a pewter sword—and we held hands and tossed them into the creek in memory of our mother. Suddenly, a strong sense of peace swept over us as a gigantic yellow and black butterfly swooped down from out of nowhere and flew over the very spot our necklaces had landed! It circled the area three times and shot up into the air with a twinkle. My brother and I looked at each other and laughed happily. "Mom is awesome!" he exclaimed.

When I returned to Cincinnati, I got my first tattoo, on my right calf—a small dog and a yellow and black butterfly, with the inscription "1954–2001" cascading from it.

Mother, I love you.

—*NoShell Lancaster,*
Cincinnati, Ohio

My Mom Said Hi

In October 1999 my stepmother Geri was killed in a tragic car accident in Colorado after visiting her son. She was a staunch believer in the afterlife. We used to joke about what we'd do if one of us passed over. We both agreed that we'd let the other one know that we were all right on the other side. Geri was interested in all aspects of the paranormal and read everything she could find on it.

Two months after her death I walked out to pick up my morning paper. I turned and saw a mist hanging from a low limb on our tree. It was about four feet long and three feet wide and floated about four feet off the ground. At first I thought it was the neighbors' dryer heat floating toward the tree, but it wasn't. I then thought it was a low-hanging cloud, but the sky was crystal clear. As I stared at it I experienced a very warm and comforting feeling, almost as if I was being hugged. As I said, it was a mist, so I could see the neighbors' front door through it. As I stared at this mist the neighbors stepped out to go to work. I looked through the mist and when I focused back on the mist it was gone.

As of this day I believe that it was Mom. She was letting me know that there was another side and she was just saying "Hi."

—*Johanna Rhoades,*
Muskogee, Okla.

In-Laws' Reunion

Since an incident that happened to me when I was ten years old, I have always watched or read stories about ghosts and the paranormal.

My mother-in-law, Julia, would say to me, "You actually believe in that stuff?"

When my father-in-law, Mike, passed away, Julia came to live with us. My son and two grandchildren lived with us too.

Julia and I would watch the morning programs together, me in my chair and her in hers. She never got over her husband's passing after 50 years together, and wished she could have gone with him. Five years later, in November 1995, she got her wish—she died from a blood clot.

One morning, two weeks after her funeral, I was watching our usual programs before getting ready for work, when a mechanical stuffed horse of my granddaughter's neighed. When I looked, it was between the cushions of my mother-in-law's chair. No one knew how it got there. I was the only one home and you had to squeeze the horse to make it neigh.

"Hi Julia," I said. "Same old, same old."

Two days later, in the children's playroom, my grandson's toy Easter bunny started to play "Here Comes Peter Cottontail." It was one of those toys with points on the bottom that have to be covered with a finger to make it play.

My mother-in-law loved her great-grandchildren, and I think it was her way of telling me, "I'm here, and you were right."

I told her to go find her husband in the light, and that we would all be fine.

I never heard from her again, and I'm glad to think she has been happily reunited with her husband.

—Mrs. M. Vicidomini,
Harrington, Del.

Family Connections

Some people don't believe in ghosts. I have never seen one myself. But I know they exist, because my grandmother's spirit has appeared to different family members over the years.

The first time my grandmother appeared was at her funeral in April 1969. My mother was sitting in one of the front pews in the deserted church after the funeral. As she sat, she remembers feeling something brush up against her. She believes it was her mother comforting her. My grandmother was only 45, my mother just 23. My mother took on more responsibility in caring for my grandfather and paying household expenses.

The second time was in late fall of 1975. We were in England at the time, in the city of Norwich. I was three years old, and my mother had not yet discovered she was pregnant with my sister.

It was in the dead of night. Mom doesn't remember if there was a clock in the room or not. She bolted upright in bed straight out of a deep sleep, terrified, knowing something wasn't right. There was a factory across the street from our townhouse. The lights were glaring through my parents' bedroom window, painting the closet door a solid white. She heard workers talking as they quit the night shift, getting into their cars and driving off.

The room was ice cold. Mom was rigid with fear. She looked instinctively toward the closet door. There was a dark outline in the light shining on it. From the style of her hair, Mom knew it was my grandmother. Looking back on it, my mother feels it was Grandma reassuring her that everything would be all right.

One of my cousins related the following story to my mother. Years ago, my cousin and her brother spent the night at our house, in my parents' bed. My parents slept downstairs. She woke up in the middle of the night to find my grandmother sitting on the bed. She was looking straight at her, smiling.

I believe I know why my grandmother keeps coming back. She died extremely young, never getting to know her future grandchildren. She has appeared to my mother in trying times to reassure and comfort her. Grandma obviously feels she didn't accomplish enough while alive. She continues to protect and guide her family.

—Kristen Voegeli,
Georgetown, Ontario, Canada

Off We Go Into the Wild Blue Yonder

Laughter and idle prattle were coming from the dining room. A three-year-old blonde girl was under the cherry dining room table, chattering presumably to the doll she was playing with. Her mother peeked into the room to make sure everything was all right and then went about her housecleaning.

Time passed and now the five-year-old girl was looking in an old family picture album with her mother. She pointed to a picture of military man and said, "That is my friend. He plays games with me and sings to me at night."

Her mother gasped in surprise.

"He has fun, shiny things all over his jacket," continued the child.

Air Force 2nd Lt. Bill Jacobson had impacted wisdom teeth. He didn't have to go on the mission that fateful day, October 14, 1944. However, feeling he had to go for his crew, he climbed into the pilot's seat of the B-24 bomber. The young pilot vowed to his wife before he left that he would always look out for her.

Two hours later over Yugoslavia, the B-24 was shot out of the sky by anti-aircraft fire. As the crew descended through the clouds in their parachutes, the Germans shot at them and Bill was killed. The surviving crew members were captured and spent the remainder of the war in a German prisoner of war camp.

When Bill died, he was listed as missing in action. Eventually, his Serviceman Group Life Insurance went into effect and his widow received $55 a month until his $10,000 life insurance was paid out. The benefit was a pittance for the life of a husband. Eventually the wife remarried, but that marriage ended in divorce. The second marriage produced a daughter, the blond child (who was me, of course).

Could I indeed have been sung to and entertained by an Air Force pilot killed in World War II?

This story was part of our family's oral history until 1985. As the years progressed, Mother started having financial problems. Because of ill health, she stopped working and was living with me. At the time, I was a captain in the Air Force Reserves. One day, I noticed a brief item in *U.S. News and World Report*:

"Widows of servicemen killed on active duty, who remarried and divorced, are eligible for Death Indemnity Compensation from the Veterans Administration."

"Hey Mom, look at this!" I said excitedly.

Mother read the blurb. "Oh, World War II was so long ago, that cannot possibly apply to me," she sighed. "Anyhow, the Veterans Administration said Bill's records were destroyed, so I couldn't document his service anyway."

After much cajoling, I talked my mother into going down to the VA office and filing for the benefit.

When Mother received compensation months later, she and I both wondered if Bill Jacobson had somehow put that blurb in the magazine from beyond the grave.

I am not knowingly sung to anymore by the deceased B-24 pilot. But during my pinning ceremony to colonel, I thought to myself, "He vowed to take care of my mother. I wonder if he is here." I saluted as the Air Force song played in the background

—Col. *Laura L. Smith, USAF (ret.)*,
Savannah, Ga.

A Christmas Gift

The green and red Christmas lights reflected in the puddles, glistening like jewels scattered across the sidewalk. Crowds of London shoppers under the protective shells of wet umbrellas scurried past, clutching purchases like trophies to their breasts. My sister Nini and I seemed to be the only ones not scanning the elegant store windows. There would be no Christmas for us this year. Our mother had died after a brief illness during the summer, and Nini and I had come to England to find her again.

The waning light clouded the signs high above our heads on the corners of the buildings. At last we found Queensbury Place. Only the small brass plaque reading "College of Psychic Studies" distinguished the stately Georgian house from its well-kept neighbors.

We were admitted by a plump receptionist and took our places in the empty waiting room. I leafed through the pamphlets stacked haphazardly on aluminum stands around the room.

"This stuff is all about apparitions and poltergeists," I whispered gloomily. "I think we're wasting our time."

"Look, we're here now. We've paid our money. Let's just see what she's like."

But I could tell that Nini too found the surroundings inauspicious. We had come all the way from Canada for a sitting with a medium in hopes of contacting our mother, but now I felt we would be terribly disappointed. While Nini and I wanted desperately to "talk" to Mummy, we were deeply skeptical. Neither of us had any patience for charlatans. We wanted proof of an afterlife. The shabbiness of our surroundings fed doubts that we would get such evidence.

We had heard about the College of Psychic Studies from an old family friend. Her son had gone missing a few years earlier. Desperate, she flew to England for a sitting at the college. The medium, Elizabeth Farrell, told our friend that her son was dead. He had been pushed off a boat during an argument about a drug deal and drowned. Soon after our friend's return to Canada, her son's body was retrieved off the coast of British Columbia.

Nini and I didn't know whether to attribute our friend's story to coincidence or to believe that her son had really "talked" to her through the medium. But we were impressed enough that we went to England during our Christmas college break to have a sitting with Elizabeth Farrell. Now it appeared that we might have made a mistake.

After a few minutes we heard the receiver clatter into its cradle. "Mrs. Farrell's ready for you," the receptionist called out.

We went up the wooden staircase to Mrs. Farrell's room. We found ourselves facing a tall, middle-aged woman in a floor-length tartan skirt, her hands folded over her middle.

"Please come in." Mrs. Farrell's voice was soft and proper. The small room was furnished with only a sofa facing the fireplace and an armchair to one side. The low ceiling added to the intimate, homey feeling. My sister and I sat down on the sofa, while Mrs. Farrell seated herself opposite us.

Mrs. Farrell leaned back and closed her eyes. "I'm going to tell you what I see and hear. All I want you to do is say 'I understand' or 'I don't understand.' Nothing else, all right?"

"Yes," we both said, and Nini reached for my hand.

For a while, the only sounds were those of the street outside and the hiss of the fire. Then Mrs. Farrell spoke. "I see a tall woman with brown curly hair. She is smiling at you. She speaks with an accent. English is not her first language. Do you understand?"

A wave of relief flooded over me. "I understand," I said. Mummy's first language was Bulgarian.

"She is looking at you with such love in her eyes," Mrs. Farrell continued. Then she leaned forward. "I think this is your mother. She passed over a short time ago, maybe four or five months ago. She wants to tell you that she is all right now, that she is not in pain any more."

Mrs. Farrell stopped, then laughed. "Your mother is dancing, whirling around the room. She says, 'Look at me, look how I can dance! My legs are working again!' She wants you to know this."

A thick lump welled in my chest and I tried to suppress a sob. Those last weeks of Mummy's illness had been so humiliating for her. She hated that she could no longer walk, that she was too weak even to get out of bed without help. Mummy had always been independent, active, and strong. Getting her strength back is the first thing she would have wanted to share with us. I recognized the tone of delight in Mrs. Farrell's voice immediately. The pronunciation was different, but the words she used were unmistakably Mummy's.

Mrs. Farrell continued. "She is an extraordinary woman, your mother. There is so much life in her, so much joy. She has a beautiful smile."

Then she paused, frowning in puzzlement. "She tells me she was a pilot, that she flew a plane. Can that be true?"

I felt almost giddy with disbelief. My mother had indeed been a pilot—the first woman pilot in Bulgaria. Photographs of Mummy wearing a leather pilot's cap and goggles adorned the walls of my parents' apartment. We confirmed what Mrs. Farrell was hearing, and she shook her head in amazement.

"Now she is holding a little white dog in her arms. Do you understand?"

"Yes," we both burst out in unison. That was our dog, Maxie. My mother had loved him and grieved for him almost as if he had been her child when he died.

"I hear the name 'Olya'. Do you understand?" My sister and I looked at each other in disbelief. My mother's name was Olga, but her Russian and Bulgarian friends called her 'Olya.'

"Yes, I understand." My voice shook.

"Your mother says not to worry about your father. He will be all right. He will marry again. He cannot be alone, your father. But she warned you before she died. Is that right?"

We acknowledged the truth of Mrs. Farrell's words. Mummy had indeed predicted that our father would marry again. Two years after our visit to the medium, her prediction came true.

Mrs. Farrell's voice softened. "She wants you to know that she loves you very much." Mrs. Farrell opened her eyes and stared straight at us. "Your mother is standing directly behind you. She is putting her arms around you and hugging you."

In that moment, the most extraordinary feeling came over me. I felt suffused with a warm glow, as if a golden light had filled my body, a feeling of love so strong that I knew without a grain of doubt that my mother was there. This was my mother's love, as strong as it had been in life, still enveloping us after death. I felt myself leaning toward my sister, as if we were being drawn together. I saw in Nini's shining face that she felt it too.

When at last Mrs. Farrell opened her eyes and ended the session, I felt like a sleepwalker reluctantly coming out of a wonderful dream. I had felt so little joy since losing Mummy, and now the sinister feeling of unreality miraculously lifted.

As we walked back to the tube station in the rain, I was exhilarated. Other people's happiness no longer seemed a rebuke of my own state of mourning. A little girl holding her mother's hand looked up at us and smiled as she passed by. For the first time in months, I was able to smile back with genuine affection.

—*Julia Weller,*
Bethesda, Md.

Okay, You Got My Attention!

I wasn't that close to my mother-in-law, Rosemary Russo. She loved to cook; I cooked only for survival. She was a hippie who occasionally let her sons raid her stash; I grew up just saying no to drugs. We were from two different generations and just didn't click. Rosemary was generally a good person and for the most part, we got along for the few years I knew her. I just always had that nagging feeling that she didn't like me because I "took" her youngest son Travis, her baby, away from her.

When our daughter Amaya was born in December 2000, Rosemary was ill and unable to experience her granddaughter's birth. Four months later she was gone. She died of heart and lung complications at the age of 49. Rosemary believed in the paranormal and I was always skeptical. That changed shortly after she died.

My husband and I started to hear the banging of pots and pans late at night, as if someone was getting ready to prepare a Thanksgiving feast. We investigated and of course there was no one in our kitchen. Perhaps Rosemary wanted her son to know she was still there, or maybe she just didn't like to be ignored.

This freaked me out but it gave my husband some comfort, so I tried to ignore it, hoping it would just stop. But what happened next made me a believer.

My husband yelled for me from the shower. I opened the door and once the fog cleared, I saw it. Our bathroom mirror was completely covered in steam except for the "R" that had been written on the mirror. I inspected the mirror and said, "If this is a joke, you better tell me now." My husband assured me it was not.

I had a talk with Rosemary that night and explained that the late night cooking and the signature on the mirror really scared me. Apparently she was listening, because that was the last communication we had. Maybe she liked me more than I thought!

—Cher D. Johnson,
Las Vegas, Nev.

A Rainbow

For most of my adult life I have believed our loved ones on "the other side" look after us. I seldom thought about this except when I had some readings by mediums, which usually were accurate and comforting. But when my husband died two years ago, I felt a great urge to study the realms of the spirit world. I read many books and planned a visit to Lily Dale (a Spiritualist community in western New York) for a reading.

Arriving at the guesthouse after dark, I went to my room after short conversations with the proprietor and his wife. In the morning, as I was leaving for a reading at another house on the grounds, the proprietor's wife asked me, "Was your husband tall, with white hair and glasses?"

"Yes," I answered.

"He walked in with you last night."

"Oh," was all I could say. I was overwhelmed with joy and sorrow—joy that he was there, but sorrow that he was no longer in the flesh.

After my reading that day by an accomplished medium—which was very accurate and uplifting—I felt that my husband was right there; that he approved of her and truly wanted me to continue studying this new belief system that transcends all religions.

After that I attended several classes at Lily Dale. On two occasions people in the classes saw my husband with me. My grief seemed to diminish when I heard of his presence. Since then I have studied, meditated, prayed, and talked with my husband. I have written a journal just for him and me. I am convinced that he has been with me often. I have felt his presence numerous times. I feel impulses to do various things—like the day I felt impelled to walk along a mountain trail we used to enjoy. Once there, I could not leave until I had the feeling he was saying it was time to go.

Something—my husband or another entity on "the other side"—has prompted me to check doors to see if they are locked as they should be, to call friends just when they need a call the most, and to look in unusual places for lost belongings. I think it is my husband, because I have such a warm, loving feeling when it happens.

At times I see past events with a sudden clarity. Though my husband was in a coma for a couple of days before his death, I realize that he directed me, through his spirit, to take care of business matters that helped a great deal after his death. Now I talk to him and inevitably get direction, sometimes subtly, but always with a feeling of love.

A very special message came on the day I cleared out our house. I was alone in the empty kitchen. I knew the sale was all right, because one day I was sure that he was saying, almost out loud, "It's time to go." But on that morning, while awaiting the final visit by the real estate agent, I sat on the floor where our kitchen table had been, and where we had shared so many moments. I asked for a sign that I was doing the right thing. Then, looking out the window, I noticed that the morning mist had risen and there was the sharpest, brightest rainbow I had ever seen. It seemed especially low, with one end of the arc anchored a half mile away and the other end in our yard.

What a blessing to know that he is on "the other side," but still with me. I am led by love.

—*Margaret K. Look,*
Nye, Mont.

He Did Come Back

On September 16, 2001, I lost my beloved companion of 25 years, Ruben Anaya, after he had surgery to remove two cancerous tumors from his stomach. His health, his heart, and his age just could not handle the trauma that goes with surgery.

My daughter Christina Carter and I went to the hospital after his daughter Debbie called me to say that his heart was slowing down. We arrived at Eastern New Mexico Medical Center about 9:30 p.m. He had just passed on; his body was still warm, and we stood there not wanting to accept it.

I called my son Danny to get to the hospital before the funeral home personnel took the body away. It was something that I thought we would never have to go through. Ruben had always been there for my children and me, a wonderful father and husband, full of energy and good ideas that kept us going. We had done more in 25 years than most married couples do in 50.

Ruben developed a number of health problems through the years. He had to have a triple bypass after having two heart attacks. He had his right leg removed due to diabetes a few years later. He did well after his amputation and got around in a wheelchair. He never lost his sense of humor. He was our hero, our knight in shining armor.

Ruben believed in the hereafter and told me several times that he would be back after he was gone. He passed away on a Sunday and was laid to rest on Wednesday. After all the calls, food, flowers, and endless parade of people, I sent everyone home to get some badly needed rest. Around seven o'clock that evening I took a long and soothing bath, as it had been a very hot day. I put on a comfy nightgown and got in bed, turned on the television, and before I knew it was sound asleep. I woke up some time later long enough to turn the TV off.

Around 1:00 a.m., I distinctly heard Ruben call me in his usual booming voice. "Hon," he said. This is how he would call me when he needed to get up or if he couldn't reach his wheelchair.

"Hold on," I answered and quickly sat up in bed, before I remembered he was gone. But there he was, standing at my doorway wearing the same clothes that we buried him in. He looked as if he had swallowed a fluorescent light—he glowed. All I could think to say was, "Look, you are walking!"

Ruben smiled at me and disappeared into a pink fog. I went back to sleep, the most wonderful sleep I have ever had. He kept his promise; he did come back.

—Minnie Alford,
Roswell, N. Mex.

Jim Returns

My husband passed away December 23, 1988. The first visit from Jim was during March 1989. I woke from a sound sleep at four o'clock in the morning when he floated in through a balcony window. His aura was so bright I was blinded by it. I remember saying to him, "Honey, please turn down your light. I can't see you very well." I asked him, "What are you doing here? Don't you know you have passed away?"

He ignored my last question. He said, "I have come to comfort you and to tell you that I love you and will always be there for you." He was sitting beside me, and he kissed me on the cheek, and I felt his hand in mine. Jim said, "Listen to me. I know you are very upset about the move you are going to make to a senior apartment complex, but there is a reason for this. This is where you are supposed to be. There are people there who need your help. You are a very good listener."

This visit was a wonderful experience. Jim was a very kind man and always helped people in need. When my son Gary returned to his apartment (where I was staying at the time), I told him about the visitation. He said, "Mom, this is all in your mind. I am going to suggest that you see a psychiatrist friend of mine."

I refused. I told Gary this had really happened. Gary said, "I have taken courses in psychology. You just wanted to see Dad so badly, you have created this experience in your mind."

I said, "No, he really was here! He held my hand and kissed me on the cheek."

Gary said, "Mom, you know you are a comedian. People like you. You make people laugh, even when you are saying outlandish things."

I know my son was trying to comfort me, so I wouldn't have to turn to the dead for advice.

I experienced several more visitations from Jim. The second time he said he just came to tell me that he was still with me in spirit every day of my life. I was curious and asked him, "Are you happy where you are?"

"I am in a very beautiful place and someday you will be here with me. Now listen to me," he said (I never would listen to him very well). "You have a lot

of work to do, so I won't be seeing you for a while."
Again he kissed me on the cheek and held my hand.

Gary thought I was under so much stress I was hal-
lucinating, but I was not taking any medication at the
time. I know in my heart Jim will be visiting me again,
and this makes me very happy.

—Margaret Elliott,
Phoenix, Ariz.

The Disappearing Check

My high school sweetheart and I were married soon
after we graduated in 1970. Being children of the
1960s, we often talked about death and the occult.
We agreed that whichever of us died first would try to
make some kind of contact.

Jerry got into drugs, much to my dismay, and we
eventually divorced in the late 1970s. As time went by,
we both married again. We remained friends after our
divorce, but kept only minor contact.

In May 1993, I received a phone call that Jerry had
died of an accidental drug overdose. I called my former sister-in-law who proceeded to tell me that Jerry's
current wife did not want me to attend his funeral. I
did not want to cause any problems for the family, so
I decided to abide by her wishes. However, mutual
friends said that was silly; I had been married to Jerry
longer than she had and he would have wanted me to

attend. I called the funeral home and they said that I could come early and pay my last respects without upsetting the widow, so I did.

Jerry's wake was on Friday, which was payday at my place of employment. I went to the funeral home and paid my last respects. I planned on picking up my paycheck afterward, but was feeling really depressed. I decided to get my check the next day, as I was scheduled to work anyway.

The next day I picked up my check during my lunch break, which was the same time that Jerry's funeral was taking place. I glanced at the dollar amount to make sure it was in the ballpark of what I was expecting. It was. The check was somewhat faded, but I really didn't think too much of it. Later that evening, I went to deposit it in the bank, but the ATM was out of order. (Thank goodness!)

The next day, Sunday, I told myself that I must get the check into the bank to cover the checks that I had mailed to pay bills. When I pulled out the check and looked at the amount again, it had started disappearing! Only part of my name and part of the dollar amount could be seen. There was no way that the bank would cash that check. I called work and they said to bring the check in and they would give me a voucher. So that is what I did, on Monday.

I gave my disappearing check to the store secretary and she gave me a voucher. By then a lot more of the check had disappeared. She said that no one else had

had any problem with their check's ink disappearing. She also asked me if that was my ex-husband who had passed away the previous week. I said yes it was. She said that she knew him also, as he was the man that came out and repaired our store's copy machine.

On my drive home, I was thinking about what she had said. Then it hit me—how crazy! My first love dies and my check disappears! His job was repairing copy machines. We had made a pact years ago to give a sign from the afterlife and he had held up his bargain!

The next day I spoke with the store secretary again. She told me that the rest of the check had started disappearing. She couldn't understand it either. No other checks had faded like that, out of 40 stores in the chain I worked for. It had never happened to me in 21 years of working there.

What are the odds of my check fading during my ex-husband's funeral? I believe that he gave me a sign of life in the next world in the way that he was most familiar with, since he repaired copy machines and printers. He still owed me a lot of money when he died, but he gave me something more precious—he gave me a deeper belief in life after death. I say I am paid in full!

—Martha Waters,
South Amherst, Ohio

The Hummingbird

My first husband Rich was killed in a plane crash. After his death, I experienced many unusual happenings. First, our favorite song came on the radio every day at lunchtime. I changed the radio station, as it made me sad. The song was on the next station, too. When I did dishes, the lid to the trash can often flew off. The stereo came on by itself, and it played our favorite song. My five-year-old niece told me she often saw a man standing on the stairs. Perhaps it was Rich. I think it was.

Periodically, the hummingbird chimes in the bedroom sounded, though there was no wind. It was evident that someone from beyond wanted my attention. Rich loved hummingbirds—he had them painted on his plane as a company logo.

A year later, I had a dream about Rich. I had been dating his friend. In my dream, Rich told me his friend was a good man, and I should give him a chance. Later, I married my present husband.

My son Ryan played baseball. He had a .000 batting average. Before his father died, Ryan played well.

One day, Ryan got two base hits. Everybody praised him. On the way home, Ryan told me: "When I was in the field, a hummingbird came toward me, then flew away."

I felt that Rich had been near to help his boy. I knew there were no bushes within about 300 yards of the field.

There were tears in my eyes as I said, "Thank you, Rich."

—Debbie Barclay,
St. Augustine, Fla.

Remember Me?

One day in 1967, I was attempting to console a middle-aged lady who was grieving over the loss of her husband. He had died eight years earlier. We were discussing life and death, and I tried to convince her that life continues in the hereafter. She gave me a quick look and then related the following story:

"You may be correct, because a strange thing happened to me after he died. Some years before, we had gone to the local garden shop to buy some flowers and seeds to landscape our new home. My husband was anxious to buy peony bulbs—but they had to be pink, only. Turned out that the owner had only white bulbs, and my husband was so disappointed. However, because he loved peonies so much, he finally agreed to buy the white ones. I said, 'Well honey, the white ones smell just as sweet—what's the difference?' He shook his head, but we left with a heavy heart.

"Peonies are perennials, and for the time we had them during the last years of his life, we enjoyed them thoroughly. He passed away five years later."

She choked up and began to cry, as she stopped to control herself. Then she said emotionally, "You know, the following year, those beautiful peonies came up pink, and have been pink every year since he died!"

—*Ethel Rawson,*
Harwood Heights, Ill.

The Purple Fields

I had been feeling depressed and homesick that day. I thought of calling Mom, but I knew she wouldn't be there. Not that day.

I was glad when Celia rang the doorbell. Not only were we classmates, but she had also become a wonderful friend. She was extroverted, open-minded, and powerful.

We had begun discussing our classes when suddenly Celia winced in pain as though she were having some kind of attack. I felt my heart jump; I feared she was about to have a seizure. She closed her eyes, lowered her head, and let out a heavy sigh.

"Are you all right?" I was alarmed by the transformation.

"Yes. . ." she replied. Her face was pallid.

"Can I get you some water? Something sweet?" I didn't know what else to do.

"Somebody's trying to call me," she uttered.

"Would you like to use the phone?" I offered, stupidly.

"No, no. Just give me a minute."

I shuffled back to the kitchen, hesitant to leave her in case she fainted. I started making coffee and glanced at the clock. I remembered what was happening back home. And Celia had told me about her mediumistic capacities. Could it be?

As I brought out the coffee, Celia was looking somewhat better but very drained.

"Sorry," she said. "Someone from beyond was trying to contact me."

I began uneasily. "Celia, today is my grandfather's funeral. He passed away three days ago, and I think they just buried him. Do you think he's trying to communicate through you to me?" I couldn't believe I was suggesting this. Nothing like this had ever happened to me before.

She nodded knowingly. She closed her eyes and returned to the trance-like state. Soon she resurfaced. "He's scared and unsure. He needs our help. What's his name?"

"Albin Kemp."

Celia took my hand. "Let's pray for him."

I closed my eyes, trying to concentrate on her words.

"Oh heavenly Father, please guide our lost and suffering brother Albin on his journey toward the light..."

We continued for a few minutes. When Celia opened her eyes, she was calm and smiled serenely.

"Albin's fine now. I saw him walking through purple fields, guided by other spirits."

My eyes widened. My grandfather had been a beekeeper in Alberta, Canada. He had loved the beautiful fields of purple clover from which his bees extracted nectar to produce honey, his livelihood.

"Why did he come so far for help?"

"Distance is not linear in the afterworld," Celia explained. "He was probably seeking refuge and felt your presence through me."

I reflected on how guilty I had been feeling about not attending my grandparents' golden wedding anniversary and three weeks later, my grandfather's funeral. Although it was impossible due to the distance and my work, I had been feeling excluded from both once-in-a-lifetime ceremonies.

Perhaps my grandfather had transcended distance to say "Goodbye," to tell me that, although I wasn't there in person, he had felt my presence at both events in spirit, just as I had felt his that day.

—*Loretta Lynn Murphy,*
Salvador, Bahia, Brazil

Grandma Just Knew

If ever there was a unique individual, it was Grandma Crawford. She was well educated for her time. Her father, William Darwin, and one of his neighbors had built their own school at Bellefonte, Alabama (the old Jackson County seat), and had brought in a schoolmaster to teach their children. It was not customary, at the time, for females to receive so much formal education. Grandma was as opinionated as was humanly possible. Not only did she entertain her personal opinions, but was always ready to express them. And if that offended anyone, it was too bad.

Grandma had a unique way of knowing things that she had no means of knowing. She was never able to explain this, other than she just knew! Her health was fragile for many years. She and Grandpa lived with us from the time I was four. Daddy's brothers lived in Mobile and worked at shipyards there. Periodically, Grandma would sit very quietly, as if in deep thought. Then, she would announce, "Roy [her oldest son] will be here this weekend." Mother would ask whether she had had a letter from him. There had been no letter; Grandma "just knew" that he was coming home. At other times, she would smile and say, "I'll get a letter from Emmett [her youngest son] tomorrow." Usually, a letter would arrive.

There were a few times when Grandma went amiss with her predictions. Once or twice, she would announce that one of her sons would be coming home, and they didn't show. However, a couple of days later, she would get a letter saying that they had planned to come, but ran into some sort of problem, such as a sick kids, car trouble, or whatever.

Grandma died in July 1960, and Grandpa was devastated. They had been married for more than 60 years. Pretty often, he would get up in the morning and announce, "Maggie was here last night." He would seem so happy on these occasions. Mother would ask if he had a dream about Grandma. That always aggravated him, and he would retort, "I didn't dream anything. She was here!" None of the other members of the family ever saw her, but Grandpa swore that he did.

During the following year, Grandpa learned that an old girlfriend of his, "Miss Mattie," was living at Woodville. Daddy and my brothers were tending some land in that area. So, one day when C.B. was going down there to check on the corn crop, Grandpa grabbed his hat and asked to be let out at Miss Mattie's. This got to be a habit. Each time one of my brothers started in that direction, Grandpa wanted to be dropped off at Miss Mattie's.

One day in September 1961, Grandpa had been to visit his friend. When he came home, he called Daddy outside to have a little talk. He told Daddy that he had decided to marry Miss Mattie. Daddy tried to discourage this line of thought by reminding Grandpa that he was 80 years old. "And too derned old to think about getting married."

Poor Grandpa moped around all the rest of the day, not saying much of anything. The next morning, Grandpa seemed highly irritated. At the breakfast table, he announced, "Maggie was here last night. And I wish she would leave me alone!"

We never learned what Grandma told him. But, whatever it was, it certainly put a stop to his romantic notions. That was his final visit to Miss Mattie's.

—Mary Crawford,
Dutton, Ala.

Daizy Talks to Grandma

April 15, 2003, started out like any other day. My wife Rowena works nights and was just getting home at 7:45 a.m. as I was getting ready to leave for work at 8:00. On the way to work, I would drop our boys off at school and take our three-year-old daughter Daizy to "Grandma's house" so my wife could sleep.

Rowena always called her mother, Pedrita Pepino ("Pedie"), in the morning to wake her up so she could watch for us and unlock the door. On that day, she got the answering machine. So she tried again a few minutes later, and still no answer. I asked Rowena to come with me and check on her mother.

After dropping the boys off at school, we went over to Pedie's house. Daizy didn't want to get out of the car. I asked Rowena to go in and check on her mom. I had a gut feeling something was wrong.

"She is not breathing!" I heard Rowena scream.

I went in and found my mother-in-law dead in the bathroom. Rowena was sure she was still alive, but I could tell she had passed on. Still in shock, I called 911. The emergency crew was there within a few minutes.

As the investigators collected information, I tried to get Daizy out of the car. She still didn't want to come out, so I got in the back seat with her. I hadn't said anything to her about her grandmother.

"Grandma die 11 hours already," Daizy said in her three-year-old voice.

I was shocked. Not only does Daizy know nothing about time and hours, she didn't even know what "die" meant, besides seeing a dead goldfish or a squished bug.

One of the investigators came out by the car, and I rolled the window down to talk with him. After answering his questions, I told him what Daizy had just said. He gave me a funny look.

"You know, according to my observations, that is just about the time it happened—10 to 12 hours ago," he said.

"Maybe Grandma visited Daizy," I said.

He agreed. "It could be very possible. Children sometimes can sense things that grownups can't. Maybe Grandma came to see Daizy after she passed on."

We didn't move anything in the home until after the funeral a week later. I was taking down photos from the wall when I noticed the clock I was about to take down had stopped at 9:25 p.m.—exactly 11 hours before the time we found Pedrita. The clock then started to work again, and is still working as I write this.

I was convinced that Daizy really had contact with her grandma. But that wasn't the end. A few days later, Daizy said, "Look Mama, Grandma is outside the window." When Rowena looked and saw no one there, Daizy said, "Oops, Grandma is gone. She went back in her box" (the wooden urn with her ashes in it).

Another time Daizy told us that Grandma was okay, and she was "cooking fish" (Daizy's favorite meal, which Grandma used to cook for her). And once Daizy said that Grandma was sleeping with her glasses on, then she took her glasses off and went back into her photo on the wall. Daizy said that she wanted to give Grandma a kiss, but Grandma said, "No, a hug only."

Daizy still talks to Grandma's photo on the wall, and even answers questions that she said Grandma asked her.

—*Dan Dehnke,*
Blaine, Wash.

Bedside Vigil for the Saved

In September 1988, my grandmother died of throat cancer. When she was hospitalized that last time, I was out of state visiting my boyfriend. She'd been in the hospital a lot the previous year for treatments and surgery, so I wasn't too concerned and my mother didn't tell me how bad off she really was. Bob was already scheduled to drive me back to college. I didn't want to ask him to take the time off work to take me to Michigan twice, as he had planned on visiting his family in the Upper Peninsula after returning me to school. So we made our trip as originally scheduled.

I was at college in Marquette when I got the news. My mother told me that Grandma had difficulty speaking and it was hard to understand her, but she was able to clearly ask, "Where's Kelly?" She explained where I was and Grandma nodded. Shortly after that, she fell into a coma and died. Classes had started the previous week, and even though it was Labor Day weekend, there was no way I could get downstate for the funeral and also complete my assignments. So I stayed at school.

After Grandma was buried, she started walking into my dreams but never said anything to me. A few weeks after her death, I had my own brush with death. I had an anaphylactic reaction to some pistachios I had eaten. I called my friend Dale and he came right over and took me to the hospital. I'd had reactions of this type before, and on three occasions they had nearly killed me. This one hadn't gotten very far, so after treatment, I was released and went back to my dorm room. Dale pulled a chair over near the bed and was going to sit with me, but the medication was very strong and was making me tired and irritable. I told him that I'd be fine and that I'd call him in the morning. He hesitantly left me alone and I fell into a drug-induced sleep.

Sometime in the middle of the night I woke up and saw my grandmother's silhouette seated in the chair Dale had occupied earlier. The drugs I was given, epinephrine and Benadryl, do not induce hallucinations, so I know she was there. I still badly needed to sleep off the drugs, so I said, "Grandma, I can't deal with this right now. You'll have to come back another time." She faded out and never returned. I figure she just wanted to say goodbye and let me know that she loved me. Once she realized I had gotten the message, there was no need for her to hang around.

—Kelly Steed,
Harrison Township, Mich.

A Reminder

I had been missing my grandmother considerably, and was writing about that fact in my journal one night. Grandma had passed away nine months before, after a long, hard struggle with lymphoma and Alzheimer's disease. I missed her terribly. We had a strong connection and were very close.

In my journal I was writing how I missed her deep, unconditional love, how I longed to feel that again. I felt a sorrow that was an ever-widening hole, and I closed the journal knowing that she wouldn't want me to feel this way. I felt something else then, a feeling that it wasn't time to go to bed yet, even though it was very late. I felt drawn to a jewelry box on my dresser that had been Grandma's.

The inside of the box smelled deliciously of her house, and I breathed in the scent to soothe my sorrows. I poked around through a pair of earrings, a butterfly brooch, and a broken section of a watchband. Then, I found a heart, made of what seemed to be shell with a gold heart attached to it. It was homemade, I am sure. I took it out and closed the box, taking the heart back to my bed. It intrigued me.

I vaguely remembered the heart on a chain around her neck, but maybe I was tricking myself into that memory's creation. I still felt that I couldn't sleep, and looked around for something else to trigger memories of Grandma. At my bedside is a small tin box in which I occasionally store a letter or two, pictures, or keepsakes with which I didn't know what else to do. Inside was a letter in Grandma's cursive, written well over a year ago. I smiled at her mentioning the magazine I was writing for at the time, and again at her thanking me for the box of clementines that she loved so much.

Near the end of the letter was something that made me gasp. "My heart will always be with you." She had written exactly what I needed to know.

We always were kindred spirits. Her prompting me to find these things proves to me that we always will be. I dried my tears and smiled. She knows I have her heart, and as a reminder I will wear her necklace, too.

—*Heather Froeschl,*
Roanoke, Va.

Communications from the Other Side

So many of us have had unexplainable events in our lives. I will describe a few unrelated mysterious happenings that I believe to be the work of angels.

A friend of mine lost her strong middle-aged son when he died of a heart attack. He had never been ill. This happened in Alaska while his mother lived in Virginia and was grieving because she had been unable to see him before his death.

I was standing in the living room of my North Carolina mountain cabin when a screen door opened and then the outer door. A big-shouldered young man, six feet tall, walked into the room and across to the kitchen, passing within inches of me. He felt solid to me and was completely dressed with a topcoat and tie. Everything was a different shade of blue; his jacket a deeper shade and his pants a different blue. His tie was the deepest shade of all. All his clothes seemed natural. I knew it was my friend's son. As he brushed past me, he walked to the end of the kitchen, opened another door, and vanished.

My friend was coming to spend some time with me. It was a five-hour drive to my cabin, so she stopped en route and stayed all night in a hotel. She arrived at my cabin the next morning. When I went out to greet her, her eyes were full of tears but she was smiling. "My son just appeared," she said, "and put his head near mine and gave me a wonderful smile. He had come to say goodbye after death. Now I feel so relieved I have seen my Jim and his beautiful smile."

He must have realized she was coming to my cabin and had expected to reach there the day before. When he did not find her the previous afternoon, he appeared again as she drove into my yard.

The next story is about a completely different strange event. Evidently, those on the other side know what is going on here. When we built my present home, there were tall windows in the front of the house. When we moved in, we discovered honey flowing down our windows. We put ice cube containers on the ledges and they were soon filled with honey. Apparently, the queen bee had made her home in the peak of my house. Then it came to me that my father, during his lifetime, often took us into the woods bee hunting. He always made sure he found the queen bee.

None of us were ever stung, but when we turned on a lamp our heads would be surrounded by a swarm of bees. Although we hated destroying our honey, we knew we had to get rid of the bees.

Then, an enormous sunflower grew up right in the middle of the windows. I have seen many small sunflowers in Florida but have never known one six feet tall with a big blossom. It grew right in the middle of our front window. My dad had adored sunflowers, as I did too. I feel that these were two examples of my father letting me know about our new home.

The last occurrence happened when my husband was managing a beautiful mountaintop inn owned by a charming and well-educated man—a nice person but extremely selfish. Shortly after his death, the thought pressed on me that I must write a message from this man. This was his message: "Imagine my consternation, when lack of volume-love put me behind all others."

I am now 100 years old, and recall these wonderful events of the unexplainable. Maybe we are given glimpses of another dimension.

—Lois Allen,
Englewood, Fla.

He Stopped the Clock

In 1996, my grandson Brandon visited us and stayed for quite a while. He occupied the upstairs guestrooms and was very happy there. He also was a great help to me, because my husband, Alfred, was very ill at the time.

After several weeks Brandon grew restless. He wanted and needed a job, so he left for southern California. As fate would have it, he had some bad luck in jobs and his personal life. He was very unhappy. I am sorry to say, he eventually took his own life.

Some weeks later, after his transition, the "touch-on-and-off" table lamps in his bedroom came on when nobody was in the room. This happened repeatedly. Alfred explained to me that it is very easy for a spirit to manipulate electrical things like lamps.

In 2001, my beloved husband passed away. During his lifetime, he had a hobby with the punctuality of clocks. For this reason he purchased an atomic-controlled wall clock. He was always very happy then the news came on exactly on time. He pointed this out on many occasions.

One afternoon a few months after his transition, I saw that the wall clock had stopped. I thought maybe the battery was low or dead, but I did not address the problem right away. Later that day, I discovered to my surprise that the clock was right on time again and functioning normally.

Now, Alfred was an electrical and mechanical engineer, so I thought that he probably had something to do with that. Knowing him, just touching some lamps would be a little too simple for his taste. He would want to do something more sophisticated—so he stopped the time on the clock.

Later, I visited my daughter Doris. When I told her about the event and my explanation for it, the lights in her living room dimmed; it was as if Alfred was confirming I was right.

I am very glad he let us know that he is okay and, hopefully, happy. For me, that is my proof of survival after death.

—Dietlind Maske,
Laguna Hills, Calif.

Daughters of Antoinette

While working as a florist in the spring of 2001, I met a customer named Antoinette who came in to order a spray of white lilies and roses in memory of her daughter. The second anniversary of her daughter's death was May 1, so she placed the order in April. That's when my dreams started.

After frequent consultations with bereaved families as a message medium, there was something natural about the correlative vocations. I became a convenient, one-stop shop, especially for spirit! When Antoinette's daughter first appeared in my dreams, I simply recorded the information and waited.

In the first dream, she was seated on my stairs in the hallway, wearing a sweet, conservative blouse and skirt.

She was tall and slender, with very short black hair. I knew she was Antoinette's daughter, and although she had no voice, her eyes beckoned for help.

The next night, I dreamed of the young woman again. This time she had chin-length hair and wore white capris and a sweater. Her skin was noticeably darker and her figure fuller. The same sense of urgency filled her sad eyes as she stood silently in my kitchen. I asked with my heart for an answer to her questioning appearances.

Before April ended, I had one more dream. This time the woman had long hair and wore a dress. She stood in my bedroom and whispered, but her voice was barely audible. All I could hear was, "Tell her."

When Antoinette returned to the shop, she was inebriated. I couldn't blame the young mother for trying to drown her sorrow, but I knew just then why her daughter's visits were so troubled. I wasn't sure how to begin, and prayed that the right words could comfort her grief.

"Your daughter has come to me three times in dreams," I said, and Antoinette's eyes welled with tears. She ignored me at first, and asked that I write three names on a message card, then pin it to the ribbon of the spray. As I did, I continued, "She can't get through to you until you take better care of yourself. Please help her, Antoinette."

"I know," she cried, "but when the time comes around, I fall apart. My girls were so beautiful!" She opened her jacket to show me the sweatshirt she had made for the memorial. All three girls were pictured exactly as I dreamt them! They were three different girls.

"You lost three daughters?" I asked.

"Well, my daughter and her two best friends were like sisters," Antoinette explained. "I called them my girls, and they called me Mom." She told me that they were all killed in a car accident while driving home from college on spring break.

"They love you so much—each one appeared to me as your daughter," I said.

"That's right," she laughed. "They're all my daughters."

I hugged her, and hoped that she found peace in my message—one that surprised even me!

—*Khimm Graham,*
Buffalo, N.Y.

I Shall Always Be with You

When I was four years old, my parents were too ill to take care of me and my sisters, Sharon and Millie, and brothers, Tommy and Billy. We were placed in an orphanage. Children were grouped by their age, which set me away from my siblings. I was heartbroken. We had never been separated before.

I did not adapt to life in an orphanage. Every time I would join my sisters and brothers, I would be plucked away and set with the other four-year-olds.

At night we would be sent to our dormitories. Each child had their own bed. It was foreign to me. I'd always slept in the same bed with my sisters. Sharon would sneak into my dorm every night. She would slip into my bed, where she held me in her arms as she sang me to sleep. She was taking a big risk, as she would be severely reprimanded for her actions.

I was adopted by the Hopper family when I was five. I was never allowed to talk about my brothers or sisters. It would be 20 years before I would be reunited with my birth family.

In 1975, I moved to San Jose, California, where Silicon Valley was just starting to take off and jobs were plentiful. One night I was restless and couldn't sleep. A small man in a dark suit was standing in the doorway of my bedroom. It did not frighten me, as I had always had that "sixth sense." Years later I learned that my brother Billy had died in his sleep on January 5, 1975. His adopted parents sent me photos. One photo of Billy dressed in a dark suit matched the man I had seen in my doorway in 1975.

If I had found my family three weeks earlier I could have seen my sister Sharon. She had suffered through cancer and crossed over before I could see her again. It was like losing my brother and sister all over again.

When I married, my husband told me I would cry in my sleep, "Don't leave me, please don't leave me." I know that is related to my memories of my sister Sharon. One night I was unable to sleep and sat in the living room alone in the dark. Suddenly, a sphere of what looked like snow was whirling around me. It looked like the crystal balls you turn upside down and it is snowing when you turn them back up.

I held out my arms, and the snow circled around and around before starting to leave. I was not aware that I had started to say, "Don't leave me, please don't leave me." I knew at once it was my sister Sharon. I clearly heard her voice softly whisper, "I have never left you, for I am always with you. You are but a whisper away."

The "snow" ascended to the ceiling and was gone. I felt instantly at peace.

Sharon visits me from time to time, bringing with her a beautiful snowfall. Billy has only returned a couple of times. Though I miss them dearly, it's comforting to know that Billy and Sharon are always with me.

—*Victoria Fugman,*
Indianapolis, Ind.

Journey to Heaven

This is a story my mother, Elizabeth Christine Wagner, related to me:

"I was a young girl when this story occurred, and the eldest of seven children. We lived in Niles, Illinois, during my teen years. My parents operated a 'truck farm.' They grew many types of vegetables and on weekends put them on the market in the city for sale.

"Mother worked very hard. She was an immigrant from France and my father was a huge man from the mountains in Luxembourg. My three brothers were bedded down in one bedroom in our meager home and we three girls in another, but our youngest sister Margaret (who was the favorite) had a cot in Mother and Dad's bedroom. She was like a delicate flower with golden curls and deep blue eyes like the skies above. Margaret was a very alert little girl and intelligent for her age. Mother doted upon her.

"Mother and Dad usually arose about five in the morning to care for the garden. But one morning Mother could not find Margaret. She was not in her cot. All of us searched for her to no avail. Mother finally walked down to the church near us for consolation and help. We all prayed hard to find her. To mother's amazement, she found Margaret sitting on the church steps; then she admonished her daughter.

"'Mama,' Margaret said, 'you don't know it, but Jesus is calling me. He wants me to come to Him and I must go.'

"Mother rather discounted all that, but whenever Margaret was missing we would find her sitting on the church steps waiting for Jesus.

"In the middle of the growing season Margaret began to look pale and listless, although she did not complain of anything. Suddenly she became very ill and Mother sent for the doctor. He put Margaret in the hospital. There she died from a ruptured appendix. The poison had immediately taken hold of her little body. Margaret had surely gone to heaven answering Jesus's call.

"Mother grieved so much after Margaret died that we were afraid for her health. One morning my brothers told me they had a secret. I was intense with curiosity. Of course my brothers were always up to some mischievous pranks, so I discounted their tales. However my curiosity won out in this instance.

"The boys swore that when they went to bed a bright light appeared on the wall. It moved back and forth and in the center was an angel kneeling as if in prayer. This was the first time I sensed some fear in my brothers.

"Now they challenged me to get into their bed and see the apparition for myself. Still doubtful of their tale, I agreed to their quest. As I climbed into their bed, I pulled the covers up to my chin, as the night was rather cool. Suddenly the bright light appeared on the wall as a circle. In the center knelt an angel with hands folded in prayer. Being the rather bold type, I immediately said, 'Ask it what it wants.' Abruptly the figure disappeared.

"The next morning I related the apparition to my mother. She looked so pale and worn. I immediately suggested going to the priest for an explanation and help. After our story, the priest told Mother the angel was Margaret praying for her to halt her grieving—that she was happy where she was, with Jesus, and she had answered His call. After that Mother dried her tears. We never again saw the apparition on the wall, but we all knew that Margaret was happy and answered the call of Jesus."

—Lillian E. Burton,
River Grove, Ill.

Sisters' Goodbye

My mother, having lost her first baby, and finding herself pregnant, took the advice of her landlady and wore a miraculous medal to the Virgin. My mother was a Presbyterian but she pinned the medal on herself and wore it until I was born.

The landlady had a daughter, Geraldine, who was then perhaps five or six years old. Once I was able to walk, Geraldine took me to St. Mary's Church in the Southside area of Scranton, Pennsylvania. When my parents moved to another area, I went to St. Mary's with new friends until we moved to a farm in the country.

When I was 12, my mother's mother came to live with our family. At that time I had two sisters, Virginia and Ruby. My grandmother saw the crucifix I had over my bed and said, "Presbyterians don't have crosses over their beds." She removed it.

"This is one Presbyterian who does," I said. So my interest in crosses grew up with me.

When I would visit Ruby and her family in Florida, we would go yard-saling and flea-marketing, and I would almost always find an interesting cross to bring home for my collection.

In March 1991, Ruby had a stroke, went into a coma, and died a month later. I was living with Virginia. There was a lake across the street from our house. The ice on the lake was beginning to break up. Right in front of our house, a huge cross appeared in the ice. I feel it was meant for me, and I took a picture from the upstairs bedroom. Ruby would often send me crosses that she found at yard sales. This cross on the lake was her way of saying goodbye.

Later, when Virginia was very sick and dying at a hospice, I would visit her daily, sometimes three times a day. Three days before she passed away I was sitting in her room. While she was resting, I became aware of a woman's hand on my shoulder.

The next day the hospice called me at home saying Virginia was slipping away. I drove there immediately. I was there only a few minutes. I told her that it was all right to leave us; I held her hand, kissed her, and told her I loved her. She breathed her last, and I continued to hold her hand.

I'm sure Virginia waited for me to arrive at the hospice. I could tell she was aware that I was there by the slight pressure she conveyed in her hand. Both sisters said goodbye to me in their own way, and I hope one day to join them wherever they are.

—*William P. Chambers,*
Tunkhannock, Pa.

"Time" for Spirits

My son, Ronnie, passed away October 26, 1981, at the age of 28. He died by suicide. Ronnie was diagnosed with bipolar disorder (also called manic depression). He had a very difficult time living his life.

I found it very hard to accept his death. I was in denial for quite some time. I would keep telling my husband Jimmy that he was not dead, he was on vacation, I knew where he was, things like that.

In December 1982, I decided to do an experiment to see if he would contact me in spirit. My husband had given Ronnie a gold watch. He felt bad because he accidentally dropped it, and it never worked again. I kept it in a small wooden jewelry box in a large trunk.

I took out the watch and held it in my hand. I meditated and asked God to make the watch tick. To my surprise, after a few minutes of concentrated meditation, the watch began to tick. The hands started to go around very slowly, then very fast. I put the watch back into the trunk. Ten days later I opened it back up again and the watch was still ticking.

I never grieved for Ronnie again as I had been doing. I had received my proof that his spirit still lived and would be with me always.

—*Margaret Elliott,*
Phoenix, Ariz.

Uncle's Visit

My maternal grandmother was born with a caul over her face and was extremely psychic. One of the many things that she predicted was the day and hour of her death—no small feat, as she was semi-comatose for the last three weeks of her life. But it is not her that I am writing about. The story I have to tell is of her brother's death ten years later.

"Uncle," as my mother and her five siblings had called him, had moved to New York from Lafayette, Louisiana, when my grandmother, his younger sister, had married my grandfather. He had lived with my grandparents off and on throughout their entire 36-year marriage and had helped them with the bills and child-rearing responsibilities. In many ways, Mother and her siblings were closer to "Uncle" than they were to their own grandparents.

He and my grandfather got along very well and continued to live together in my grandfather's home for seven years after my grandmother's death, until my grandfather sold it. Then Uncle decided to go back to Louisiana for an extended visit while he decided whether to live there, close to the siblings he hadn't lived near in decades, or in New York, close to his many nieces and nephews and their children.

He left shortly after my baptism in September 1970 and said he'd probably be home in time for my first Christmas. However, this did not come to pass. One month into his stay and the day after watching another sister's daughter get married, he had a heart attack and died. He was only 70 years old.

Uncle died quickly and peacefully it seems. He was getting out of bed, possibly on his way to the bathroom, and just died with one foot in the bed and one foot on the floor. One of my aunts had passed him as she too was on the way to the bathroom and went back to her room so that he could use it first. When she came back 15 minutes later, Uncle was in the same position, and still warm. It was 3:15 in the morning.

Mother had just put me back in my crib after feeding me. I was two months old and quite prompt about my feedings. She hadn't counted on my waking up again until around seven. She has always been a poor sleeper once awakened, so she turned on the radio and was thrilled that one of her favorite programs, the *Long John Nebel Show*, was on. She loved his stories of the paranormal, even though she was usually a bit spooked by them.

My crib was on the other side of the room. She heard a loud whisper that said "Mommy" and even felt breath in her ear. She went to check on me and walked down the hall to check on my ten-year-old brother. On the way back she realized that I couldn't whisper anything at the age of two months and that she would never be able to hear or feel my brother whisper "Mommy" in her ear from a room on the other side of our three-bedroom, two-bathroom apartment! She was quite spooked.

Then the phone rang. It was 3:20 a.m. My aunt Lita gave her the sad news and asked her to call my aunt Peggy, to whom she was not speaking.

Mother dialed Peggy's number. Peggy picked up the phone and said "Chita?" (Mother's name) before Mother could say anything. Mother told Peggy the sad news and then told her that she thought I might be possessed. When my aunt asked why, Mother recounted half of the tale—the other half my aunt had filled in for her. The same exact thing had happened to Peggy. She heard "Mommy" being whispered in her ear and also felt the breath, went to check on my nine-year-old cousin Tony in the next room only to find him sound asleep. They both heard this at 3:15 a.m.—the exact time of Uncle's death.

Mother went into my brother's room, woke him up, and insisted that he come sleep in the bed with her. He was annoyed, but she was not going to sleep in the same room alone with me: the creepy, whispering infant!

Approximately a month later, Mother and my aunt called the *Long John Nebel Show* to recount their tale. They were told that sometimes, when a person dies, he is greeted by his mother and that either Uncle was greeting his own mother or he was reaching out to his nieces, whom he had helped raise and who were now mothers themselves, to say goodbye. He may have chosen the word "Mommy" to guarantee that he had their attention. Man, oh man, did he get it!

Either way, this story has been bandied about my family for almost 33 years. I find it amazing, but not at all surprising.

—*Jocelyn Brathwaite,
Bayside, N.Y.*

My Friend Butchie Remembered

My belief in the afterlife is stronger after an episode that happened to me more than 30 years ago. In 1968 I worked at the Miami Herald alongside an elderly lady, "Butchie," who became a good friend of mine. We used to discuss religion and afterlife experiences, and we both said that if one of us died, we would try to contact the other. In 1970 I married and moved away, and we lost touch.

On the night of December 20, 1971, we received a call from Butchie's husband Charles. He told us that Butchie had died of cancer that afternoon, and he was trying to let everyone know. I was upset; I never got to say goodbye to her! I hadn't spoken to her since I moved away.

That evening I went to bed as usual, and was close to dreaming when two wrinkled fingers nudged me out of my sleep. I woke up and looked around my bedroom, but no one was there. I checked, and no one in my household had been in my bedroom.

I knew it was Butchie—she always kept three fingers on her headset wire, while using her other two fingers to nudge me to get my attention when she was on the phone.

I had another strange experience in the 1990s when I went to Boston with my family on vacation. My husband and I had been fussing in our motel and he left with my daughter to go to a car show. While he was gone, I started to feel the worst pain in my backside, leaving me breathless. It didn't let up, and the motel manager called for an ambulance. I could hear my mother saying, "It will be all right honey, just hang in there."

I was taken to the hospital and discovered I had a kidney stone. Our vacation was cut short. When we returned home, I visited my mother in her little town in Florida. Mother asked me, "What happened to you on the trip?"

I told her and she said, "I knew something was wrong and I felt it." She asked me what day it happened and I told her. She told me that was the day she "sensed" something had happened to me. She couldn't quite figure out what it was except that it was a bad premonition. She is gone now, but I never thought about us being that close until it happened so far away.

—Helen Forgay,
Lithonia, Ga.

Mary Comes Back

When I was very young, I had a little playmate named Mary. We used to play all kinds of games together. Then Mary died at the age of ten.

As the years rolled by, I often thought of Mary dying at such a young age.

After I retired, I became a school crossing guard. One day when all the kids had crossed, I was ready to go home. Then I saw another kid coming down the road. I waited until she got closer. She looked different from the other kids. She had no school pack, and was dressed like little kids were back in the 1940s.

When I saw her face, I thought I would fall over. It was Mary, my little playmate who died 58 years ago. She said hello, but I could not speak.

Then the most amazing thing happened: Mary's mother's face began to form to the side of hers. Her mother died at the age of 80, but when I saw her face she looked to be in her 20s. I tried to ask a question, but before I could speak she vanished. I could not believe what I had seen.

—George Stone,
Cambridge, Ontario, Canada

My Friend Mel

I met Mel Kay at a church meeting. He was a father figure to me. I shall always remember how he read the Lord's Prayer most every Sunday morning. Mel was one of the most kind, loving, and caring individuals I have ever known.

Mel took sick with a life-threatening disease. It was heartbreaking to see him fade away like an autumn leaf.

Months later, Mel made his transition. When our friend Irene called and gave us the news, I became very depressed. We knew he was going, but I was sad at the thought of never seeing him again.

When I am depressed, I sleep. I went into the bedroom, closed the door, and went to sleep for two hours.

As I was waking, someone sat on my bed. Thinking it was my husband, I turned over to see what he wanted. I could see no one there, yet it felt as if someone sat on my bed. Startled, I sat up. Then I heard these words: "It's all right."

At that moment I felt relieved. All sadness left me. I recognized Mel's voice. This proved to me that there is life after death, for there is no death. There is only Spirit that makes a change.

—*Willie L. Watkins,*
St. Augustine, Fla.

Mary Ann's Spirit

It was Friday afternoon, April 19, 1974. My wife Mary Ann was lying on a recliner chair in our front room when she died. I came home from work about four o'clock and went to see how she was feeling. I saw that she was dead, so I called Walter and Edwin, who were outside, and Sherman, who was in his room. When the boys had come home from school, they all thought their mom was asleep. I told them she had died. We went into the front room to see her. She looked like she was in a very peaceful sleep.

After calling the funeral home, I called Stanley, Jr., who was in college in Rochester, New York, and Mary Ann's mother Esther Bailey to tell them the very sad news.

That night, the three boys and I were drained emotionally. We needed to have some dinner and I wanted to get out of the house. I suggested we go to McDonald's. They thought that was a good idea, so off we went. The four of us sat in a booth and we each had a tray of food. Sherman had crooked teeth and wore a wire retainer, which he removed when he ate. He didn't have the retainer box with him, so he placed the retainer on his tray. When we were through eating, we put the food wrappers and cups in a large container and went out to the car.

Just as I started the car, Sherman said, "Dad, I don't have my retainer."

We all went back into the restaurant to look for it. I told the manager what was lost and asked him for an empty garbage container. While Walter and Edwin looked around and under our booth, Sherman and I took each piece of paper and garbage out of the container where we had disposed of our trash and put it into the empty one. We inspected each handful of trash, but we didn't find the retainer.

I thanked the manager for his help. We washed our hands and went out to the car. Sherman was upset because he knew the retainer cost $100, and it was his fault that it was lost.

As I started the car, Sherman said, "Dad!" Look at my lap!"

There was the retainer on his lap. I knew at once that Mary Ann's spirit had taken it and put it there. We were very sad, but it made us happy to know her spirit was with us and telling us she was okay.

—*Stanley R. Colson,*
Indian Harbor Beach, Fla.

Ghostly Apparitions

Ever caught something in your peripheral that looked suspiciously alive? That wisp of vapor or a lick of shadow; that blink of light or a suspicious reflection; that glob of something immaterial or something seemingly too symmetrical, too ordered, or, well, too intelligent to be anything less than a spirit?

For those select few that have seen the coup de grâce—a solid, unmistakable apparition, that delivers that killer blow on doubt—could there be any plausible explanation outside of the paranormal? How willing would you, the reader, be to accept something so far beyond the 21st century paradigm?

In 2003, a Harris Poll confirmed that a staggering 84 percent of respondents believed in the survival of the soul after death. With this alleged survival come a slew of simple, yet lingering questions. Where to next? In what form does the spirit endure? Are our bodies merely vehicles for transcending the material frequency? Do spirits pass into a different vibration or into an alternate dimension from that known to the living? For those too troubled by their passing to accept it, could they actually reach out to the living in lurid and convincing displays of immortality? Or are they trapped somewhere within their own conceptions of purgatory?

For anyone that has encountered the dead first-hand, the answer is a simple and glaring, yes. If seeing is believing, then how could one ignore having seen something so rare, so glaring and so deliberate? These are just a few of those real-life accounts, where reason meets reality and where reality gives reason to believe the unbelievable.

Go Toward the Light

Shortly after looking at my pickup truck, which I had advertised for sale, my friend John Turner was murdered.

Just about the time of his demise, I decided to go for a walk. As I opened my front door, the streetlight across from me blew out. I then walked down the hill, where I bumped into a friend of mine named Paul Kjorne at Martin Luther King Park, a couple of blocks from my house.

John, Paul, and I were all members of the Minnesota Street Rod Association. As Paul and I started to talk about John's murder, something made us look up at the streetlight across from us. We observed a phantom figure with its arm outstretched, reaching toward the light. It was only the upper torso, tapering off into a smoke or a mist, and was a translucent, grayish white. Almost simultaneously the streetlight exploded and went out.

As this happened, Paul's mouth popped open and his eyes bugged out as he shouted, "Paranormal!"

I left Paul and headed home. When I got a quarter of a block from the next streetlight, it too exploded and burned out. I thought to myself, "Was this John's spirit telling us he was heading toward the light and that he was now all right?"

—Dr. Michael Denis Michaelson,
Minneapolis, Minn.

An Image from Beyond

Even though I lost my biological father before I was born, I've seen evidence that there really is still life after death. When I was around 13 years old, I found myself at my aunt's apartment along with several of my cousins. Out of the blue, and partially out of boredom, someone got the idea that we should play a game. I knew right away that this couldn't be too good, but I had no real idea just what it was I was about to get into.

The game required a dark room, a mirror, and a few reluctant participants. Though it was in the middle of a sunny day, there happened to be an unused room in the very center of the apartment. There were doors on each of the four sides of this room and no windows. We grabbed a mirror from the living room and sat it on the floor, propped against the wall. I had no idea what was going on or what to expect.

The cousin who had suggested the game gave instructions, telling us to close our eyes, spin around in a circle, and chant. We had decided to use the name of my deceased father. I didn't like this game to begin with, but that was going too far for me. Still, I was curious. After all, it was just a game. I came to find out that, like many other "games," it was more real than I expected.

We closed our eyes—at least, the others did. I chose to crack mine open a little bit every few seconds or so. You can imagine my surprise to actually see an image coming from the mirror! It was a glowing form, like a person standing upright. As frightened as I was, I couldn't just stand there and stare. I rushed for daylight, then stood gasping, glad to find myself out of the dark.

Don't believe me? Then I dare you to try it for yourself.

—*Cameron T. Brown,*
Heflin, La.

The Pig-Like Creature on the Dumpster

Children are usually taught that there are no such things as ghosts, goblins, or things that go bump in the night. Naturally, as a kid, I would go out with my friends looking for these monsters.

I saw a lot of strange things growing up, especially when I was seven years old. I think this is when I became aware of my sixth sense. It was the third time that I saw something paranormal within the same year.

I used to ride my bicycle all over the apartment complex where I lived in Spring Valley, New York. My friends and I would explore the nearby woods. We would go searching for monsters and be ready to attack with our fake swords and shields.

One time, I noticed these peculiar branches in the shape of a pig's foot. They kept appearing everywhere I looked. It was a foreshadowing of what I was about to see. Upon exploring these woods, I thought I saw something flash by in the corner of my eye. I heard a snorting sound, and I saw a small figure dash into the night. I could only see its back. At first I thought it was a midget or a leprechaun, but I couldn't get a very good look at it.

I returned several days in a row, with no luck in finding this creature. I searched but never found it. I still had a feeling it was lurking in the woods. It was hiding, getting ready to appear when I least expected it.

Weeks passed by, and then one late night, I had to take the trash to the dumpster. This was next to the wooded area where I had seen the monster. I remember it was a full moon that night. A lot of paranormal activity happens during this time as well as two days before a full moon and two days after. Also, there is an increase in activity during lunar eclipses, solar eclipses, and meteor showers.

When I threw the bag of trash into the dumpster, I thought I saw something from the corner of my eye. I heard a grunting sound in the woods. It seemed to be coming from behind a bush that moved.

At this point, I was scared, so I got on my bike and frantically rode away. I told myself not to look back. I couldn't take the suspense any longer, so I turned around and looked back at the dumpster. I couldn't believe what I saw. Standing on the dumpster, I saw the creature walking.

It was hideous. It looked like its upper body was a pig and its lower body was a goat. Actually, the head looked more like a wild boar. It was all hairy and it had a short snout, long, sharp bottom teeth, and pointy ears. It had sharp talons and hoofed feet.

It was standing upright, and it looked right at me. I screamed, jumped on my bike, and sped away. I kept looking over my shoulder to see if it was following me. Thank God, it wasn't. Needless to say, I did not return to the dumpster for months. I made my brother take the trash out.

Once again, I thought it was my imagination, but then I remembered I had seen the old lady and experienced the poltergeist earlier that year. I told my friends in the neighborhood about the creature. They went looking for it but never found it. I stayed away from the dumpster and never saw it again, but I will remember it for the rest of my life.

—Lisa Yorio,
Albuquerque, N.Mex.

My Visitor

This happened to me when I was in high school 26 years ago, and I remember it like it happened yesterday.

I went to high school on the Choctaw Reservation, at Pearl River in Philadelphia, Mississippi. The Choctaw Reservation is one of the most active places for spirits that I have ever known. The reservation consists of seven communities. On Friday afternoons the kids who lived in other communities were bused back home for the weekend. I came from an out-of-state tribe (Chitimacha), so I always stayed the weekend with the others who were from out of state.

The dormitory was a very big and scary place to me. At that time I was very afraid of spirits; now, knowing more about it, I am not. On this particular weekend, how I managed to be in a room alone is still a mystery to me. I usually made sure that I was in a room with my brother or cousins.

When I was young, my brothers and cousins used to scare me and tell me that monsters were going to come and get me at night. So I would pull the covers up over my head, thinking that, if the monsters couldn't see me, they couldn't get to me.

On this particular night I was awakened by fighting for the covers. I was trying to pull them over my head, as something very strong was trying to pull them off me. I had my eyes shut tight, with the covers under my chin, struggling to get them over my head. I was terrified and didn't know what to do. After a few minutes of this I decided that I was going to open my eyes and see what it was that was trying to pull my covers off me.

When I opened my eyes, the covers fell back onto me and the bed, and this huge, smoky white hand went shwooop! like it was being sucked into a vacuum. I was so afraid that I jumped out of bed and ran down the hall to where my brother and cousins were sleeping.

They were all asleep, of course—it was the middle of the night. I ran into their room screaming about this big white hand, and not making much sense to them at all. They put me off and said it was just a dream. But I know with every fiber of my being that it was not a dream.

At the time I was very afraid of it, but now I feel that it was a good presence and feel that maybe there was something I was supposed to learn from this. Like I said earlier, I have never forgotten it, and I have only talked about it over the years to very few people. I feel in my heart that when and if I am supposed to know what it was or what it meant, Creator will let me know. If anyone else has ever had an experience like this, I would sure like to hear about it.

—*Walter Twofeathers,*
Charenton, La.

Séance on New Year's Eve

My interest in the unexplained began shortly after my eighth birthday. I read anything that I could get on the supernatural, psychics, and strange events. I believe that nothing is really beyond the natural. We will explain everything once we figure out how to measure and quantify it.

Having séances seemed like a fun way to entertain my friends, so I bought a black candle and followed a ritual I found in a book. I have always believed that some people are mediums who can call on the spirits of those who have passed on; I just did not think I was one of them. Therefore, in order to impress and scare my friends, I devised ways to cheat. A piece of hard candy in my mouth could be quietly spit out at an appropriate time to create a "spirit noise" across the room. I could also free one of my hands by tricking the people on either side of me to hold only one of my hands. I was then free to create "spirit touches" in the dark.

I started these entertaining séances a few months before at my sister's birthday party. Everyone enjoyed my performance and kept asking for more. My method was to call on the spirits of dead famous people, such as George Washington, Abraham Lincoln, John F. Kennedy, and Marilyn Monroe.

On New Year's Eve 1972, when I was 12 years old, my parents went out with friends, leaving all the children at our house to celebrate together. We were provided with plenty of snack foods and soda.

Around 8:00 p.m., someone asked me to perform a séance. We all sat on the floor in my brother's bedroom around the lit black candle. Including me, there were nine people present: Gail, my best friend; Sean, my brother; Vikki, my sister; and my friends Scott, Holly, Dale, Barry, and Dawn, who were all siblings.

I called on various deceased famous people and used my tricks. Then Gail asked if I could call on her mother, who had died in a car accident about 12 years before when Gail was only a year old. She never knew her mother, having been raised by her paternal grandmother.

Everyone present said that I should do this, so I agreed, although I thought it might be upsetting to Gail if nothing happened.

After I called on Gail's mother, a light appeared in a corner of the room. It was like two wheels, rotating, one inside the other. Everyone saw it and panicked. I said "Break the circle," and we all let go of each others' hands. Then someone said, "It's still there."

At that point, mass hysteria started. The candle went out. Everyone was trying to get past everyone else to leave the room, but no one could seem to get to the door or the light. I had to disentangle myself from several people and crawl to the light switch and door. I managed to reach up and flick on the light. Then we could no longer see the light wheels.

Everyone rushed out of the room and went downstairs to have some soda and snacks and celebrate the New Year. They all refused to talk about what happened. Some of them will not talk about it even now, 32 years later. They all refused to ever have a séance with me again.

—RayNice J. Hoffman,
Reading, Pa.

Skeleton Key

"C'mon, open," I muttered.

I fiddled with the rusty lock, but the knob wouldn't turn. Sighing, I charged the cabin door, which felt more like brick than wood as I slammed into it.

"Ouch! Honey, I accidentally locked the door!"

I bounded down the porch and stood by my boyfriend Brian, who was hunched over a roasting rack of marinated chicken.

"I don't have the keys with me," Brian answered.

"You don't?"

"Nope. They're inside."

He examined the cabin's perimeter for an open window. "There's screens in all of them!" Brian complained, his fingers clawing at a stubborn screen.

"Nice going, Deb!" our friend Ron chided as he took a swig of beer. He belched obnoxiously.

"Pig!" I scolded, the two of us snickering. Our shared sense of humor made him one of my dearest friends.

"All right," Brian interrupted, "who's driving to the ranger's station?"

"I'm drunk!" Ron shouted proudly.

"Well, I'm cooking dinner," Brian pointed out.

"Okay," I relented, "I'll drive, but someone's coming with me."

As I slid into Brian's car, Ron climbed into the passenger seat. Within minutes we arrived at the state park road and turned left. An oncoming truck's high beams flicked on and off.

"Hmm," Ron observed, "your brights aren't on."

As the truck passed us, I glanced to my left, hoping to catch a glimpse of the driver. Instead, my eyes darted to a sudden brightness up ahead. It appeared to be a man standing in the middle of the road. *What the hell?* I thought, only seconds from reaching it. *Please don't cross.*

I screamed as I watched the man step toward my lane. Quickly swerving to the right, I felt my stomach flip. Eight white knuckles stretched my skin as my fingers choked the wheel.

With the brilliance of an exploding sun, his body flashed before me. His footsteps stopped and he, or it, floated above the road. For a brief second, I was awestruck by a tall, translucent figure. I felt immobilized, depleted of my breath by this nonhuman form. Its disproportionate, faceless body drifted toward me, until the glowing mass was inches from my door. Then, like a windswept mist that moistens one's skin and swiftly evaporates, it vanished.

"Did you see that?" I asked Ron.

"What the hell was it?" he responded.

"At first I thought it was a person. But as we passed it, I knew it wasn't."

"It looked translucent, like an apparition."

"It looked like a ghost! I could have stuck my hand right through it!"

We coasted into the ranger's station parking lot.

"We should have asked those people in the truck," Ron said. "They pulled over—I looked back after they passed us."

After receiving a new key from the ranger on duty, we drove back to the cabin and unlocked the door. Then we returned to the station to drop off the borrowed keys. The ride back was unusually quiet. It was still early, but the road was dead.

When we returned to our lodging, I snatched our camcorder and started my interview. "Ron, what did you see tonight?"

"I saw a ghost, some kind of apparition."

"Really?" Brian broke in.

I concurred and rehashed the story. The three of us hardly spoke during dinner. My mind was jammed with supernatural thoughts. I sat between the two men. Halfway through their second post-dinner drink, we reconvened our discussion. The fire continued to burn, along with our curiosity.

"He seemed to be wearing a top hat," I explained. "My grandfather always wore those." As I brushed some ashes from my cuff, I made a discovery: I was wearing my grandpa's old green flannel shirt. I looked up and gasped.

"That's weird," Ron said. "My grandfather wore hats."

"Really?"

We held each other's gaze, letting the silence blanket our group. While my pupils blurred into the fire's orange flames, my mind sculpted my grandfather's image. His striking features shimmered through the dust, and the canvas of time lifted to unveil a forgotten treasure: my grandpa's face, grinning under that thick head of silver hair the way I remembered him.

"Maybe they're watching over us," Ron surmised, searching my face for answers.

"Maybe," I responded, my voice hushed, "they wanted to tell us we'll be okay."

"I hope so," Ron added wistfully.

Then Brian spoke up. "Guys, I didn't want to tell you before, but I found the key."

"Where?" Ron and I asked.

"As soon as you left, I found them in my pocket."

"They were there the whole time?" Ron cried.

Brian offered an apology. "Sorry, guys. They weren't there before, but after you left..."

"Don't be sorry," I told him. "For some reason, we were meant to see that."

"I guess we were," Ron agreed. "What are the chances of that?"

Sighing, I shrugged my shoulders. Maybe it was fate. A rush of adrenaline bubbled in my blood. Were our grandfathers trying to contact us, or did we intercept a message sent for someone else? "Only God knows," I whispered as I fell to one knee and made the sign of the cross. I shifted my eyes to the night sky, sprinkled with tiny glints of light. Perhaps it was written in the stars.

—Deborah Nadolski,
Cheektowaga, N.Y.

The Calico Cat

Cally is a short, fat female cat that started showing up at my house in January 2002. She showed up at the same time every day, so we assumed that her owners let her out when they got home, and being that she was quite fat, she was just looking for an extra free meal. We have fed a number of stray cats over the years and have always kept an extra bag of food on hand.

About the end of February, Cally started staying and not leaving during the day. Sometime during March, we started seeing the wispy outline of a woman passing through the kitchen, nothing clear, just a vague outline. This did not strike me as too odd, being a member of various paranormal groups. I have seen many strange things and have had poltergeists in the house in the past.

One mid-April day, I was looking out of our sliding glass doors onto the deck where the cat was looking back at me. For about three seconds, a full apparition of a little old lady appeared right on top of the cat. I saw her as clear as a real person standing there. She was very frail, had her hair in a bun, wore a long-sleeved, full-length, dark print dress, and looked like she was at least 70 years old.

Not knowing what was going on, but having some idea, and having some training with dowsing, I got out my pendulum and started asking questions. I learned that the cat had come from no farther than five miles away. The ghost was the cat's owner, who had died in January. I also learned that she was hanging around because she was concerned about the cat's well-being.

Wanting to confirm what I learned, I started asking around and found out that the widow "Smith" (not her real name) had lived about three miles from me, had died in January, and fit the description of my apparition exactly. I also found out that her son took over the house and threw everything out. That could explain the cat's fear of males. It took some time, but it has since accepted me.

I let Mrs. Smith know that we would be taking good care of her cat and we would be taking it to the vet along with ours for shots next week. I told her it was time to cross over, go to the light. We have not seen her since and the cat is still here. I guess living by herself, that cat was very important to her and, as fat as it was and used to being indoors, very pampered. I feel she could not cross over until she knew that her cat was going to be taken care of.

—*Thomas M. Ginther,*
Alton, Va.

The Real Little Men in Black

One day in 1942 I was asleep, alone, in my bedroom. The room was pitch-black. At the time I was five years old and lived with my grandparents in Duluth, Minnesota. During the early hours of the morning I awoke and looked toward the end of my bed. On the other side of the brass end-rail was a three-foot-tall figure dressed all in black and wearing what looked like a bowler hat.

How or why I could see this entity in total darkness was beyond me. Putting my head under the covers several times didn't do anything to make him disappear. Finally, I fell back to sleep, and in the morning he was gone.

The man in black did not frighten me, but from the little I knew of reality, I felt he was certainly out of place. That was the only encounter I had with the little guy, though I had several out-of-body experiences since then that may or may not have been related to the encounter.

During my recent Christmas visit to Salt Lake City, Utah, I spoke with my 20-year-old granddaughter Tiffany about my experience. She has had some paranormal experiences, so I asked her if she had ever seen what I saw. She told me that she had two similar visits; the first when she was seven years old, and another when she was 17. Like the visit I had, she also saw them in her bedroom. She said they were wearing what appeared to be bowler hats, were dressed in black, and it happened in total darkness. Unlike me, she was a little perplexed by the happening.

Tiffany also said that she occasionally sees figures out of the corners of her eyes that are also dressed in black, but of considerably greater height—but when looked straight on they were not there.

I'm sure we are not the only ones graced by such visits.

—Bill MacDonald,
Elk River, Minn.

An Encounter with a Shepherd and Ha Ha

This incident happened when I was in Viet Nam in July 1969.

My wife Irdean (Dean) and two kids stayed in our mobile home on land owned by her parents in the country near Hollister, North Carolina. On one side of the mobile home was a garden, and after that was a large forest that stretched for miles and miles.

I was winding down my tour at Tan Son Nhut Air Base and had started shipping some of my things home. Dean worked on the night shift at a textile plant near Whitakers, North Carolina, and when she finished she headed for home.

There was one area on this country road (Route 4) that she drove through where there were not very many homes for a long distance. One night when she approached this area, there appeared to be a dense fog on the road. As she drove into it, something told her: Don't drive too fast. You don't know what is around the curve.

Dean slowed down, and to her surprise there was a herd of black cows on the road. Some had bells around their necks. She considered blowing the horn to make them move off the road, but something said: Don't blow the horn, just blink your headlights from bright to dim, back and forth.

Dean did this, and the cows parted to both sides of the road to clear the way so she could drive through. Oddly, she did not hear their bells ringing or their hooves on the hard surface.

As Dean came through the last of the cows, she saw a "person" standing on the left side of the road. He wore a robe made out of a burlap material with a hood covering his head and shading his face, and he held a stick in an upright position in his right hand. The sight made her think of biblical shepherds watching their flock, or Moses carrying the stick or rod when he led his people out of Egypt and parted the Red Sea.

As Dean drove beside this person, she cautiously rolled her window down an inch to speak to him. He spoke to her in a mechanical voice: "My cows got out."

"I see they did," she replied, and since he said nothing else, she continued on home.

(Seven or eight years later when *Star Wars* came out, she identified the mechanical voice of the "shepherd" as being identical to that of Darth Vader.)

Dean drove home without further incident and went to bed. However, about 11:00 p.m. that night and the following nights she heard the dogs outside, by the side of the trailer facing the woods by the kitchen, barking like crazy. After a while their barks turned into frightened whimpers, and then they got deathly quiet. Shortly after that she could hear something breathing very heavily outside, starting at the same area and then coming by the first, second, and third bedrooms. Slowly it moved around the back of the home, then to the front towards the kitchen. There the sounds would taper off.

Dean asked her mother what she thought it was. Her mother replied it was just a deer.

Dean's sisters and brothers visiting from out of town spent a night with her and heard the same noise. "What in the world was that?" they asked.

"It was just Ha Ha," she replied.

I don't think any of them spent more than a night with her.

Dean was concerned for the kids, but not afraid of "Ha Ha." Her nephews and nieces living close by were concerned, however, so they took turns spending the night with her.

One night Dean's niece stayed; both of them slept in the third (master) bedroom. As before, the dogs started barking, then whimpered and quieted down when Ha Ha made its presence known by the heavy breathing. Dean had had enough and decided to confront the unknown visitor by shining a flashlight on it when it came to the side of the trailer from the first bedroom. But a tug of war ensued over the flashlight. Dean's niece was afraid to offend the "haint"; Indian legend maintains that if you angered a ghost you would never be right anymore.

Dean relented, but decided to at least look out the window when it came around. In the bright moonlight, her astonished eyes saw something like a ball of wool the size of a basketball, floating about a foot off the ground. In the upper portion was something like a light shining on the ground in a back-and-forth pattern.

Dean pulled her niece out of bed and asked her to look and confirm what she had seen. Dean's niece looked and described the same thing she was seeing.

After it came to the front side of the home, the apparition and the heavy breathing faded away. That was the last night Ha Ha came to visit.

In a couple days, Dean picked me up at the train station and told me about it. Out of curiosity I went to the side of the home facing the garden and woods, where Ha Ha would come. I found one of my brother-in-law's beagles under the side of the home. The dog had died with his eyes open, looking toward the woods.

Sometimes when we experience things there is never an answer, and this may be one. However, sometimes things happen that confuse you or give an answer we don't understand.

In August 2007, I was at the MUFON Symposium in Denver, Colorado. Looking over various vendors' tables, I came across one who had statues and molds of various beings. I asked what they represented, and the vendor said they were people from different planets.

I left her table, but something told me to go back and look again. Lo and behold, this time I found the statue of a being fitting the description of the person my wife saw with the cows in 1969. I asked the vendor what it was, and she replied that he was from Nebulon. Then I told her about my wife's experience. We were both amazed. Sometimes truth is stranger than fiction.

—*John T. Richardson,*
Camp Springs, Md.

Waving Apparition

An interesting event happened to me in October 1937, when I was about ten years old.

I was living in Bemidji, Minnesota, with my family, consisting of myself, my parents, and three younger brothers. I slept in the front bedroom with two of my brothers. I slept in a single bed, while by brothers shared a double bed.

One night, I found myself awake for no apparent reason with what appeared to be a female figure, five to six feet tall, standing beside my bed. The figure was facing me and standing near the head of my bed. It seemed to be covered from head to foot with a white gown, much like a wedding dress. It was a complete cover for her body and I could not see any of her face, nor any of her skin. I thought it was just a dream. I closed my eyes and went back to sleep.

The next night, the figure appeared again in the same place. This time it was waving a white cloth over my head and I could see a bare forearm and hand. The skin was that of a Caucasian, while the rest of the figure was covered by the same clothes as before.

I stared at this image with disbelief and became determined to prove to myself that this was not really happening. So I made a grab for the hand that was waving the white cloth to prove that there was nothing there. To my great surprise, my fingers grasped the cold, hard, and smooth hand of a human woman. For some reason, I made no attempt to call out to awaken my brothers. I put my head under the covers and immediately fell asleep.

I have never experienced an encounter similar to this since then and I have no idea what the figure was attempting to communicate to me, if anything. I would like to hear if other people have had similar experiences.

—James W. Buchanan,
Duluth, Minn.

3

Dream Visitations

Some dreams are harder to shake than others, received more as visions hatched by either deep unrest in the observer's psyche, or potentially by the actions of unseen forces or entities. For whatever reason, these dreams embed themselves in the fabric of one's psychical inquisition, giving clue to the unknown depths of the universe and one's own unique place within.

Yet what could these dreams actually mean, and wherefrom were they spawned? As though dreamt from the white peaks of reason and truth—glimmering with some ethereal quality of omniscient rightness—these dreams seem to leave the observer either laden with questions or sated with assurance.

The rush of thoughts precluding any one of these episodes can leave one sliding back on one's heels with wide eyes. In the end, however, one universal outcome seems to transcend the mass: Despite debating origins and validity, these dreams are always extremely impacting and transformative for the observer—emotional and quaking.

Indeed, sometimes people see messages or signs in their dreams that seemingly manifest themselves in reality. Yet others dream with metaphorical insight into the psyche or with inert emotional scruples. While others, still, might be awakened just in time to stop a terrible catastrophe, having been aided by a disembodied word, usually from a deceased loved one.

It seems that like the dreamworld, we know so little about the afterlife. So how could people, in good conscience, put down the possibility that somewhere, perhaps, a portal exists between the plane we visit in our living sleep and the plane we occupy in our eternal rest? Here are just a few of those accounts to ponder.

A Summer Dream

After looking at a family photo album this past holiday season and seeing pictures of my Uncle William, I was prompted to share this true story.

It was August 1982, and I was 16 years old, when I experienced my first symbolically psychic dream. My dream occurred on what was to be the last night of my Uncle William's life.

Fondly known as "Uncle Willie," he was my mother's favorite brother, and my favorite uncle. A soft-spoken man with a kind disposition, he was always there for my mother and other family members through good and bad times. He helped my mother financially as she faced the difficulties of raising three children in a low-income housing project. My uncle was a genuinely good-hearted soul.

My dream, consisting of two separate scenes, seemed like a puzzle whose pieces did not fit. First, I saw a faceless, genderless ice skater performing a perfect, repetitive figure-eight pattern on a flawlessly surfaced sheet of ice. The scene took place in twilight, and the incessant pattern of the skater was so smoothly executed it was mesmerizing.

The image that appeared next after the skating scene faded out was that of a shiny, blood-red apple—vaguely reminiscent of a human heart in shape and size—dangling vulnerably, in midair. It seemed ready to drop at any time. My dream ended with the apple still suspended in the air.

The next morning came, and it was a hot Saturday, August 8. The telephone rang, and a little while later I heard my mother cry out in a grief-filled voice. I immediately ran to her side. Uncle Willie's wife, Claire, had called to tell us that Willie had died in his sleep the previous night of a heart attack. As I silently listened to the painful news, I felt an odd sense of positive confirmation and relief, which I know was connected to the dream that I had the night before.

The ice skater performing the repetitive figure-eight amid spectacularly reflecting ice (representing Heaven's illumination) was representative of my Uncle Willie. August 8 (eighth month, eighth day) was the date of his passing, and he was the last born of eight siblings.

As for the shiny apple hovering in midair: Apples had always been Uncle Willie's most famously beloved food since childhood. Given its color, shape, and size, it likely represented his heart as well.

The precise timing of my dream, along with the details encrypted within and the novel, confirmatory feeling I felt upon hearing the news allowed the puzzle pieces of a summer dream I had to fit together.

—*Esther C. Seltzer,*
Brooklyn, N.Y.

A Promise Kept

My dad and I had a very special relationship. He was not only my parent; he was my teacher and my best friend. He encouraged me when others put me down, claiming that I could do anything as long as I believed I could. His faith meant a great deal, and through his trust, I accomplished things that the doctors claimed were impossible for a person in my physical condition.

I was born with a severe case of cerebral palsy. The best prognosis for me was that if I managed to survive the wrath of my brain damage, I would never be more than a vegetable, oblivious to the world around me. "Put her away in an institution and forget about her," was the advice offered my parents. Fortunately, both Mom and Dad turned a deaf ear, deciding they would defy all odds and help me accomplish as much as possible.

The hours of therapy were endless and painful, but slowly progress was made. I could sit up, feed myself, and speak. None of this happened overnight, but my parents were diligent, and for their efforts I grew healthy in body, mind, and spirit.

Despite everything I managed to do, there was one thing I couldn't do and that was walk. Dad and I both loved the ocean, and our greatest desire was to be able to run on the beach together. This was our dream, our prayer, and our catalyst for never giving up, even in the hardest times. When the pain was most excruciating, Dad would gently wipe my tears and whisper, "I promise—one day we will walk beside the ocean with the wind in our hair."

He repeated this promise a million times over the years, but at his funeral, I sat in my wheelchair. Daddy was gone, along with our dream. I missed him so, but life went on. I thought of his unfulfilled promise often and felt maybe I had let him down by not trying harder to walk.

A month after he died, my friend Cathy spent the night at my house. We went to bed around twelve and I fell into a wonderful dream. I was with my dad, and we were running on the beach holding hands. It was all so real! I could feel the wind in my hair, the salty spray of the sea kissing my cheeks, and the cool grainy sand between my toes. And I could hear my Dad's deep hearty laughter as we ran like children at play, skipping over the rocks and dancing in the waves. It was everything we had dreamed of—everything he had promised.

In the morning, I couldn't wait for Cathy to wake up so I could tell her my dream. I felt so wonderful, better than I had since Dad had left. She sat on my bed listening intently as I described everything. I wanted to re-live every precious moment, over and over. When at last I was through with my story, Cathy stood up to help me out of bed and into my wheelchair. As she pulled back the covers, her hands flew to her mouth and she whispered, "Oh, my God!"

My eyes followed hers. It took me but a second to realize what I was seeing on my sheets and feet—there was beach tar everywhere! My feet and toes were caked with the black sticky substance. There was no other explanation for the state they were in, except that Dad had indeed kept his promise.

—*Sunday Uher,*
Fort Lauderdale, Fla.

A Wake-Up Call

The death of my mother, Viola Laris, left a devastated family that had been so close. It happened in the early 1970s. A few weeks after her funeral, on a summer afternoon, my older sister Angela Pane, a heavy smoker, decided to take a short nap on the couch, something she usually never does. However, she was extremely exhausted and needed to relax.

She lay down and lit a cigarette, with the intention of taking a few drags and putting it out. Of course, the obvious occurred: she dropped off to sleep quickly, still holding the lit cigarette in her hand.

Nobody was at home, and it was quiet and peaceful. Her husband, who was a surgeon, was at the hospital. Suddenly, she dreamed that the phone rang, which woke her up with a jolt. The cigarette was about to burn out and onto her body when she jumped up and frantically put it out in the ashtray next to her.

She ran quickly to answer the phone. Mother's voice screamed: "Put your cigarette out!"—and she hung up.

"And then I woke up," said Angela when she told us the story the following day. "I was standing by the table and looking at the phone, which was still on the receiver. I don't know how that happened, but that phone call from Mom saved my life...I could have burned to death."

—Ethel Rawson,
Harwood Heights, Ill.

Funeral Message

My aunt, Lillian Hein, had been living in a retirement home for a couple of years. She was neither chronically ill nor in frail health; she just didn't want to live alone any longer because of a fear that she might fall, break a bone, and be unable to get up. We visited her when we could and found her to be quite happy in her new home. She even enjoyed her roommate.

On July 11, 1999 (the birthday of Lillian's husband Charles), I had a dream that it was actually September 16 (my husband's birthday), and I was helping my cousin select a burial outfit for her mother, Lillian. Tears streamed down my cheeks with each garment we inspected.

The next morning I woke up with a feeling of dread, and during breakfast I related the details of the dream to my husband. He sighed, "What a way to celebrate my birthday." I told him the impressions left from the dream were so strong I felt I should immediately ask for a vacation the week of September 16. I encouraged him to do the same.

A few images in the dream puzzled me. For example, the position of Lillian's bed was changed and the windows in the room lined the opposite wall, which was different than in real life. Also in the dream, my aunt did not have a roommate.

One image in particular was very clear. I found individually wrapped, hard peppermint candies in the pocket of the jacket we chose as part of Lillian's burial outfit. I distinctly remember holding them in my hand and passing them to my cousin.

The details of the dream and what actually transpired are eerily similar. After Aunt Lillian became ill and it was clear to her doctor that she would not survive, she was moved into a quiet room at the end of the hallway. This was done out of respect so the family could sit with her in her last hours without being disturbed by other residents. The room was on the other side of the hallway and so the bed and windows were opposite from the original room.

After she passed away and arrangements were being made, the logical choice for the funeral was September 15; however, because there were other funerals in the small town, the minister was not available. The service had to be scheduled for September 16.

After my cousin selected the burial clothes for her mother, we found hard peppermint candies in the jacket pocket.

Walking to our car after the graveside service, my husband turned to me and sighed, "What a way to celebrate my birthday."

—*Danette Hein-Snider,*
Council Bluffs, Iowa

The Hidden Message

It was a cold, gusty day in November 1998 when my husband came home and announced he had been laid off from his manufacturing sales job.

"That's all right, honey. We'll be okay," I said, hoping to disguise my worry. Who was I kidding? Bills needed to be paid, and I was trying to supplement our income with a freelance-writing career. Although I asked God for assistance, I never knew that I'd receive help from someone I hadn't seen in over 20 years.

Over the next few weeks, I wrote in the evenings after working as an executive assistant during the day. With Christmas only two weeks away, I also spent time reminiscing about the Christmases of long ago when my grandparents were still alive. One night as I lay in bed, I remembered opening gifts with them below a funny-looking tree that my family called "the bush." This was because my grandfather always bought a tree that was too tall for the living room and would saw off the top. But as comical as that evergreen was, its fragrance drifted throughout their stucco house as the colored lights warmed its boughs. And it glowed again in my dream that wintry night.

In the haziness of the dream, my mother opened my grandparents' front door after knocking several times. She called out to them but received no answer except the echo of her own voice. My father and three brothers wandered through the house looking for them to no avail. I knew that my grandparents had passed away, but why didn't they? Suddenly, cheerful shouts rang out from the kitchen and I rushed over as fast as I could. Sitting at the tiny kitchen table was my grandfather, surrounded by my parents and brothers.

"I can't stay very long," he said. "Grandma should be arriving soon, though."

When my grandmother entered through the nearby hall, we grew very still. "I have something important to show you," she said, beckoning me to follow her.

Out of the house we went and into the vast sky she flew, a trail of stars shooting past as I ran along the sidewalk below her. Where could she be going? I turned into a lot that emptied onto an unlit street. The door to a one-story building at the center of the block was wide open, and I could see my grandmother's silhouette beneath a dimly lit bulb. Upon entering, I saw piles of books lying undiscovered on rows of wooden tables. She handed one of them to me, but the dream ended before I could see the title.

I awoke with a feeling of unreasonable amazement. Something strange had happened, but I could not distinguish what the strange thing might be. As silly as it may sound, I was frustrated that my grandmother might be keeping a secret from me. I scarcely even noticed when the bedroom door slid open and my husband appeared.

"I thought you overslept," he said.

I glanced at the digital clock on my bedside table, relieved that it was 7:30 a.m. Thankfully, I had enough time to get ready for work.

"I had the weirdest dream," I said, rubbing my eyes as I slid out from under the covers. But the dull morning light was already peeking through the curtains, allowing the vision to fade.

When I began work that day, my co-worker Mary Misic told me about an armoire she had bought over the weekend.

"Where did you get it?" I asked.

"The Lake Forest Resale Shop," she said, beaming. "Can you believe it? It was practically brand new when I bought it!"

"Do they have other antiques?"

"Well, pretty much used stuff—some in good condition. I can't believe you haven't been there," Mary said. "Just walk up Deerpath Road, and when you reach the gas station on the corner, make a left. After that, it's a little confusing." She scribbled directions on a sticky note and handed it to me.

"Thanks," I said. "Maybe I'll walk over during lunch."

At noon I ate a turkey sandwich at my desk and strolled outdoors afterward. The salt-strewn walkways didn't look very inviting, but with directions in hand, I strode to the corner. A quick glance at Mary's handwriting told me that she didn't write down the shop's address. "Brown building next to hot dog stand" her scrawl seemed to read. Hard-packed snow crunched beneath my boots as I ventured down Oakwood, a street I had driven down many times before. As I walked along, I had the peculiar sensation that someone was following me, but when I turned around, no one was there. Instead, what I saw was the parking lot in my dream!

I stared ahead in disbelief at the same building that mesmerized me the night before. The only difference was the sign reading "Lake Forest Resale Shop" above its cloudy window. The smell of grilling hot dogs filled the air as I walked toward the wooden door.

Once inside, I felt a stab of disappointment. The room was nothing like I had envisioned it. There were racks of old clothes and kitchen items scattered throughout the cramped space, but not the rows of wooden tables that brimmed with books.

My curiosity led me to a set of tall bookcases on the far wall at the back of the store, where a few patrons were thumbing through worn paperbacks and old hardcover books. To my surprise, I found a book called *Saved By the Light*, about a woman's near-death experience. This must be what my grandmother wanted to show me, I mused.

Satisfied, I was about to leave when a copper mold caught my eye—the kind that used to hang on my grandmother's kitchen wall. As I held it in my hand, I happened to glance at the bookcase next to me. There sat a Holy Bible bound in beautiful maroon leather. I set the mold down to touch the gold lettering on the cover and flipped the book open. I was astonished that someone had penciled in the cost of only one dollar. Unable to resist, I purchased both books.

When I opened my mail that evening I received the usual junk and a few rejection letters from editors. One, however, was from an editor at *Quaker Life*, a Christian magazine located in Richmond, Indiana. He was responding to my query letter. "Please send us your essay using verses from the New International Version of the Bible," he wrote.

If there was one thing that I hadn't noticed about my new Bible, it was the version, but one quick glance proved that I had the right one.

"Gary! Come quick!" I screeched, waving the letter over my head. But the house was empty.

With my husband undoubtedly out on a job interview, I went to work on my essay. However, it was only after countless revisions that I sent it out. When it was published several months later, I had the newfound confidence to write many stories afterward—an ability I never dreamed I had.

Although I will never be able to prove that my grandmother intervened on my behalf, I know that this mystical experience will remain with me for the rest of my life. And one day, I will thank her for revealing her hidden message.

—Joan S. Voss,
Libertyville, Ill.

Grandma Said Goodbye

The death of my mother, Marvel Lucille Deason, was quite a shock to the family. When she passed June 30, 1993, at the age of 64, we were given no warning. What had first been diagnosed as a pulled back muscle was revealed on an MRI test as bone cancer. We were given these results the day I arrived for my annual visit to my parents' house in Lakewood, California, from my home in Concrete, Washington. My mother died 11 days later, during which time the family took shifts so that one or more of us was with her at all times to try to ease her incredible pain in any way we could.

My beloved grandmother, Martha Victoria Deason, followed my mother in passing only two months later on August 20, 1993, at the age of 87. As she'd lived a very long, full life and went very easily, we were not too surprised. But my immense grief at the loss of my mother worked to prevent me from grieving Grandma Deason. As I lived out of state and had just returned home, I missed her funeral. This was especially sad for me as Grandma Deason and I had been very close.

Grandma Deason was one of those blondes they tell jokes about. Always talking and laughing, repeating the same old stories over and over, which tended to drive the rest of the family crazy. All except me—I'd kind of listen with half an ear, and it was the sound of love, like the soft patter of rain on a window to me.

Since she lived her life alone for the most part, after working as a single woman supporting her mother, my great-grandmother Dora Rath, and my father Charles Bryan Deason, I made a special point of taking her to lunch regularly, after which we'd window-shop at the local mall.

Once I took my six-year-old son Dane Andrew Young and a friend of his with us. As I paid for a purchase they went ahead, and to make a long story short, Grandma's senile dementia (which was increasing her confusion as she aged) resulted in her and the children "losing" me at the mall for over an hour! I found them, with the help of friends I ran into about the time I was getting panicked. I managed to calm myself, and after reuniting we all had a good laugh.

About two months after Grandma Deason died, I awoke from a very vivid, realistic dream, like none I'd ever had before. I had tears in my eyes and on my cheeks as well. In the dream, I was sitting in a chair next to a bed. Grandma Deason was sitting up in the bed. I didn't recognize the room—it was like a room in an old folk's home, but not like the one she'd stayed in. We were visiting together, laughing and reminiscing over old times. Then we thanked each other for being in each other's life, we kissed, hugged, and cried at the parting. I woke up in the midst of this emotional goodbye.

I was still shook up as I walked into the front room and told my husband, Hank Young, about my experience: "I think I just told Grandma goodbye."

I would have thought it was just a dream, except for what followed. . .

As Grandma Deason had been in a nursing home for several years when she died, she had no belongings to speak of. They'd all been sorted and given away years before to her loved ones and her church. Imagine my shock when an hour or so after arising that day, I got a phone call from my dad, telling me to be on the look-out for a check he'd just sent. It was a check for $1,000 from a policy left to him by Grandma Deason—she'd asked him to share it with all four of us grandkids!

As I got off the phone in shock, I looked at my husband and said, "I think Grandma just said goodbye to me!"

—*Diana L. Young,*
Concrete, Wash.

Near-Death and Out-of-Body Experiences

Near-Death and Out-of-Body Experiences transcend time, culture, ethnicity, and geography. Even the ancient Egyptians had a ritual for entombing the living in an airtight casket, pushing mortality to the very edge of its limits. Through trial and error (and regrettably, the death of numerous slaves during the experimentation phase) the Egyptians were eventually able to discern the line between life and death in terms of oxygen deprivation.

Seeing this as a great agent for divining about the world, the Egyptians enforced the existence of the soul as a separate entity from the living body. With this observation, the Egyptians unwittingly gave birth to a debate that occupies medicine into the current age.

The question remains, is a near-death experience a truly spiritual experience or is it nothing less than (a sometimes drug induced) hallucination generated by the brain to smooth away the jarring transition between life and death?

For those who have walked the line, truly, between the living and the ever-after, the vivid nature of these experiences convincingly portrays a world beyond. While definitive support for these claims is sometimes hard to come by, other times, accounts of what transpired during the observer's death—e.g. what the doctors conversed about, who was present and what they were wearing, where they stood and how they accomplished reviving the dying—are provided by the observer in perfect detail. Then what? It seems that at some point the angle FATE offers most coherently summarizes the findings. Fact just isn't enough sometimes. Faith, on the other hand, spans the gap in the greater scope.

Voice from the Other Side

When I was a five-year-old in 1957, I spent the summer with my three siblings at our grandparents' lakefront home. It is a time that is still vivid in my mind.

My aunts, uncles, cousins, and parents would come on the weekends. The family would ski, swim, and picnic at the lake.

Learning to dive deep for rocks one late summer day, water filled my ears. I was prone to earaches, and the pain was excruciating by nightfall.

That evening, I slept on a sectional couch covered with plastic, with a hot-water bottle for a pillow and wads of cotton in both ears. I could smell fleeting scents of mildew mingled with roses. A fever had settled into my body as I tossed and turned, trying desperately to find a bit of comfort. Muffled sounds of creaking plastic kept waking me up; at times my tender skin stuck to it.

Near dawn, exhausted, I felt myself leave my body. I entered into a dark, dark void. In front of me appeared a long, glowing silver cord, about an inch or two in diameter. Tiny fibers radiated out of the cord like a piece of jute twine. I felt its texture, reaching up with both hands and running my fingers along the line. Moving my hands to the middle of the cord, continuing to feel with my index fingers and thumbs circling the line, I pulled slightly on both sides.

To my right, I heard the sound of a man's distorted, metallic laughter: "A Ha...Ha...Ha...Haa..."

I immediately stopped what I was doing and made a beeline back to my body. Fighting hard to get back in, my fear and panic increased as I struggled, paralyzed. I paused for a second to listen as I slammed back into my body.

I felt my head and heart pounding. Shaking, I jumped up. The house was quiet. Trees moving in a slight wind made dancing figures on the walls, shadowed by the twilight of the rising sun. Sitting there, afraid to move, transfixed by the images, I listened to the sounds of my own breathing, praying that thing I heard wasn't coming after me.

As I grew older, my out-of-body wanderings continued. Each time I realized I was out of my body, the same panic I felt in the void would return. In my late 40s, after years of agonizing over that experience I had as a young child, I went to see a psychic (Charles Tiemann) to ask who, what, and where that place was.

"How did it feel?" he inquired.

"It was peculiar," I said, "echo-like."

He sat there, staring. "What was it?" I pleaded, feeling the fear rise as I looked into his blank eyes.

All of his spirit guides were talking at once, he said. He tried to explain. Though I was little and full of pain, I couldn't just break the cord that attached my spirit to my body—that was not allowed.

"That voice you heard was probably one of your guides, trying to teach you a lesson," he concluded.

Was it the pain in my ears or the plastic on that sectional that made me want to take a quick exit from this world?

Now, when I catch my wandering spirit out chasing rabbits in the garden, or staring up at the star-filled moonlit sky, I remind myself I am here to have a material experience on this plane, in this body. But still some nights I wonder: Was that voice I heard in the void friend or foe?

—*Tara Voler,*
Lemont, Ill.

The Gift of an OOBE?

One day in 1964, when I was 11 years old, I went out of body at midday while completely awake. It was effortless and appeared to be choreographed by someone discarnate, beginning to end. But who was it? And how did they know it was exactly what I needed?

My family had just settled into a new home in Fresno, California, after our second move in several years. Acutely shy, I was having major trouble making new friends. Once again I felt uprooted and uncentered. My only old friend and link with the past was my cat, a sweet and snuggly old calico.

Then I discovered her body on the side of the road, crushed by a car, and I sank into a deep depression. Trying to make things easier, my mother let me adopt a kitten. Foolishly, I picked one from a litter of barn cats. They were Siamese, with beautiful markings.

They were all completely wild and had to be viewed in a cage.

And Jennifur stayed wild. I brought her home in a cage and let her out in an unused storage room, three rooms down from my bedroom. Jennifur hid behind the boxes, yowling whenever anyone came into the room. When I tried to coax her out, she hissed at me and darted from box to box, moaning in terror. She was probably wondering why I was waiting so long to kill and eat her. Every time I passed her room, and thought of her hiding all alone, crouched in a corner, I felt awful.

About mid-afternoon on a Saturday, right after an attempted visit, I lay on my bed crying silently. I missed my friendly old cat so very badly. She'd always been such a comfort whenever I was feeling low, snuggling and "purr-rumbling" right in my face. The more I thought of her, the emptier I felt.

I remembered finding her cold, still body on the side of the road. No more purrs, never again. At that, I started crying so hard, I really felt like I'd never be able to stop.

But after only a half-hour or so, I wore out. Staring blankly at the ceiling, in a strange, dull, spacey state, I felt removed from all feeling. It was such a relief.

Then I began to rise.

I wasn't trying to. And in fact my physical body wasn't moving at all. But "I" was rising, and it truly felt as though someone was pulling me up and out of my body, just as if two physical hands had reached under my upper arms and hoisted me into a sitting position. Then, without any warning, they shoved me headfirst right through the wall.

I barely felt its mass as I passed through—it was nothing more than a light pressure. Then I was over on the other side, hanging in the hallway.

I floated uncertainly, not quite touching the ground. I realized I couldn't be in my body. At the same time, I felt just as real and alive as I had inside it only moments before. There was no change, I was just not gravity-bound any longer.

But why was I floating out in the hall?

It seemed like I was waiting for something to happen. I felt a tug from the far end of the corridor and turned to look.

Jennifur had just entered and was heading my way. And I just knew she was going to my room, a place she'd never even seen. I could feel her purpose.

Maybe it was due to the surprise I felt in seeing her there, but something snapped me backwards through the wall and right back into my body again. I sat up just as the kitten rounded the open doorway to my room and jumped up on my bed.

Holding my breath, I successfully teased her into playing with a ribbon. Later she allowed me to touch her. That afternoon, she finally decided to trust me. And Jennifur soon settled in as the family cat. Things got better, and my depression lifted. I didn't think about it for years.

But lately, I've been considering all the implications the experience suggested. I'll never forget feeling the hands under my arms, dragging me out of my body. It seemed someone knew Jennifur was coming to visit me just then, and wanted me to see her. Did the same being also send her to visit me? The timing was so perfect as to be suspicious. And if so, why? To make me appreciate the fact that it was a "set-up"?

And was it only coincidental that in order to get a sense of perspective over the passing of my old friend, I'd been given a taste of temporary death myself?

It was almost as if someone was telling me, "See, going out of body didn't hurt you a bit, did it? So cheer up! Your old kitty is just fine too, wherever she is!"

But the most encouraging consideration was that there were beings on the other side so compassionate as to be drawn in to help in such a small matter as a little girl grieving over a dead pet.

—*Valenya,*
Hoopa, Calif.

Out and About

My odd story began on a Saturday morning in May 2004. For years my grandfather (Karl Christenson) had been bedridden and had to have someone constantly looking after him. That someone was usually my grandmother (Myrna Christenson). But my mother decided to give her a break and took her out for the day. It became my duty to look after Grandpa.

I walked over to my grandparents' house and took a seat next to his bed. All was well until an hour after I arrived. Grandpa started complaining about pain in his lungs. I called the ambulance and they took him away to the emergency room.

In a panic, I called my older sister, Sarah, to come over. When she arrived I told her what had happened. We sat at the kitchen table and waited for my uncle Ken to get home from work. When he got home, we told him about what happened.

I remember saying, "Okay, we need to come up with a way to tell Mom and Grandma that Grandpa is not here."

My sister, being a kind of joker, said, "We'll say he's out and about!"

It was about then that we started hearing strange noises from the garage, like big, heavy footsteps. We stayed silent as the footsteps made their way from the garage to the tiled floor of the kitchen. My uncle got up and yelled "Get out!" in the direction of the footsteps. And as fast as they had started, the noises stopped. We checked all around the house, but no one was there.

Finally, Mom and Grandma came home, and we gave them the "out and about" line. Of course, they didn't buy it, quickly figured out what happened, and immediately got back in the car and went to the hospital. We discovered Grandpa actually had a collapsed lung.

When Mom and Grandma came back from seeing him, they handed my sister and I a slip of paper. When they saw Grandpa, he couldn't talk, only write. The paper was covered with answers to simple questions. I read over the paper. A chill crawled down my spine as my eyes ran over one answer. In my grandpa's scratchy handwriting it said, "Yes, I was out and about."

I asked my mom what the question had been. She said she had asked if he had gone out of his body when he was at the hospital. He wrote that he was "out and about." That was something that my grandpa never said before.

Was Grandpa actually the one causing the footsteps? Was he really listening to what me and my sister were talking about? I'm not sure, but I'll never think of that simple three-word phrase the same way again.

—Megan Senate,
Carson City, Nev.

An Amazing Bond

July 4, 2004, was a day to celebrate. It was a typical hot Texas summer evening; the temperature was hovering in the upper 90s. My husband and I were having a couple of friends over. We planned on having plenty to eat, and then popping a few fireworks and having a couple of drinks, nothing too elaborate.

My daughter, Christina, who is 15, was spending the night with a friend, so we would have the place to ourselves. Christina and I have always been close. We have that special mother-daughter relationship that so many mothers long for. I've always considered myself extremely lucky to have such a unique bond.

Rod, my husband, started the barbecue pit around six o'clock. Our friends arrived shortly after. They brought a 12-pack of beer and a bottle of tequila. I'm not too much of a drinker, but I thought I'd have a few.

We sat outside in the backyard at our backyard picnic table. The big oak trees were providing plenty of shade and there was a gentle breeze blowing. We were talking, telling jokes, and genuinely enjoying each other's company. Christina joined us, as her friend was not picking her up until eight o'clock. I had a couple beers as we laughed, having a good time. Rod hadn't started cooking the meat yet, so I told myself I better not drink any more until I eat something.

I brought out a deck of cards and we started playing games. Peer pressure, I suppose, made me drink a few more beers. Then Rod opened the bottle of tequila.

"Go cut up some limes and bring the salt shaker out here," I told Christina.

She looked at me, puzzled. Christina knows that I don't normally drink, much less hard liquor.

"Go on, Christina, do what I say!" I told her.

She reluctantly followed my orders and went inside.

I could feel myself entering into a faded world of drunkenness. I had no control to stop at this point. Christina emerged from the house with a plate full of neatly sliced limes and the salt shaker from our kitchen table.

"Mom, are you okay?" she asked.

"Yes, I'm fine," I replied.

My friend poured some tequila into the shot glass that he brought.

"You first, Pam," he said, and handed me the glass. I took it.

Looking into the amber liquid, I was thinking I shouldn't drink it, but quickly dismissed that thought. I grabbed a slice of lime and poured some salt onto my hand.

"Lick it, slam it, suck it!!" everyone started chanting, and I did.

"Mom, I'm leaving! Kari's here to pick me up!" yelled Christina, who was coming out of the back door. It must have been eight o'clock already. How the time had flew by!

"Okay!" I said. "Be careful"

"Mom, are you sure you're all right?" she asked.

"I'm fine, just go ahead and have fun," I slurred.

But I was not fine. My body felt tingly and as I got up to walk Christina out, I realized that I couldn't walk straight.

"Mom, I really don't want to leave you, I've never seen you like this," said Christina, fully concerned about me.

"Christina, I'm okay. I'll have something to eat in a little while, and then I'll be all right," I replied.

"Okay, Mom, but if you need me, or if something happens, you better call me," she said, sternly.

"I will," I lied. Then she left.

Food at this point was not a priority for me. I remember having at least two more shots of tequila and walking inside the house saying, "I'll be right back." That was my last memory of that night.

I was floating. I looked around. I was in my bedroom. My vision was not clear; it was blurred, like when a sick child wakes you in the middle of the night and you jump up to tend to him. I looked down and I saw myself lying on my bed a couple of feet below. I was vomiting profusely. Then I heard a male voice behind me.

"You're dead," the voice said. "You had too much to drink tonight and you died of alcohol poisoning."

I was overcome by a complete state of shock and terror. "No!" I cried. "I can't be dead! My daughter needs me; please, I don't want to die," I pleaded with the unknown voice, over and over again.

Ring. . . ring. . . ring. . .

I opened one eye and looked around, confused. The red numbers on the clock by my bed read 9:00 a.m. I was lying in my bed, fully dressed, in a pool of vomit. I lifted up my head. It was throbbing. There was dried vomit pasted to one side of my face.

Ring...ring...ring...

"The phone." I thought. I stumbled out of bed and went to the phone.

"Hello," I mumbled.

"Mom! Are you okay?" It was Christina, and she sounded hysterical.

"Yes, I'm okay; what's wrong?" I asked.

"Mom," she started, her voice sounding a little less frantic after hearing mine. "Last night I was asleep. About 11 o'clock, something made me jump up out of my sleep. I don't know why, but I had this over-whelming feeling of sadness come over me. I felt like something was wrong with you—like something had happened to you. So I woke up Kari, we sat down, joined hands and started praying. Over and over again, we prayed: 'Please, God, let my mom be okay; please, God, watch over my mom and don't let anything hap-pen to her.'"

My eyes filled with tears as the memory of what I experienced the night before resurfaced. I realized this all must have occurred around the same time.

"Christina," I said through my sobs, "I think you saved my life!"

The next day, I called my pastor and made an appointment for my daughter and I to see him. We told him everything that occurred. Although he would not say one way or another if I truly had an out-of-body experience, he did say that he had heard of stories like ours. He also said that Christina and I have a unique bond, similar to that of twins.

I feel extremely blessed to be alive. I suppose I am here for a reason. I thank God every day for giving me such a wonderful daughter and for giving me a second chance at life to spend with her.

—*Pamela D. Cruz,*
Austin, Tex.

Grandma's Staying

On October 10, 1968, the telephone rang. The message was horrifying. My grandmother, Marie Handley, had been in a terrible car accident in Palatine, Illinois. My dad was given the message to come as quickly as possible. His mother was being given her last rites, and her chances of survival were slim. Dad scheduled a flight from Tucson to Chicago.

The day of the accident had a special significance—it was my tenth birthday. A week before the accident, I had a dream of a woman in blue floating in a starlit atmosphere. The pasty white lady flashed many images of future events and people. The last thing I remembered clearly was the message to pray for some-one who would get hurt. I ignored the message until the day of the phone call. I felt somewhat responsible for the accident. I was reluctant to tell my folks, but I managed to share my weird dream.

My dad arrived at the hospital out of Chicago the next day. He viewed his mother. Her head was the size of a basketball with bruises. He hired the best brain specialist at the hospital. The doctor placed tubes in her head for drainage. She was in a deep coma.

Later, Grandma said she had dreamed of a beauti-ful garden. She walked up to a big wooden door. She saw many colorful flowers and trees. Three people stood at the entrance of the open gate. Joe (who was driving at the time of the accident), her mother Sarah, and her husband Tom were all coaxing her to enter. All three had passed on, but she had no knowledge that Joe had died due to her deep coma. Her willful personality pulled her away from the gate. She stepped away and decided not to enter. The door closed, and she woke from her coma.

The hospital staff was surprised. They were in dis-belief that this 68-year-old lady had survived such a traumatic injury. Grandma recovered fully. She did not need speech or physical therapy. She walked out of the hospital as if nothing happened. She lost a few teeth, and that was the only loss besides her boyfriend driv-ing the car.

After the accident, Grandma kept all her most famous qualities. She was the best pie-maker even though she wore coke-bottle glasses. Her pace kept all of her children and grandchildren running behind. She was cunning, and loved to play chase games with the children.

Nanny might have been welcome to join the other side, but she made the choice to stay longer. Nanny lived six more years after the accident, until her third bout with cancer took her away from us. Maybe she is happy, because I don't dream of her any more. I just remember her cozy little bungalow in Palatine, Illinois, and her panic reaction to be the first down in the basement during a tornado siren. She would be 102 today if she had survived.

—*Peggy Handley Johnson,*
Lee's Summit, Mo.

Unconscious Memory

In the following lines I wish to share a most astonishing incident told to me by my nephew, Dr. S. J. Gandhi, a physician at the Amey Hospital in Panvel, Maharasahtra State, India. The story concerns the experience of a patient at his hospital.

Mrs. Rajwant Kaur had been diagnosed as having a thyroid disorder. Her husband was a truck driver of very ordinary means. Mrs. Kaur had been losing weight gradually, and had become quite a skeleton. She also had a swollen neck and was advised to have surgery.

During the surgery, it so happened that one of the surgeons cut the wrong artery by mistake. The doctors were unable to stop the bleeding, and the patient was given a blood transfusion to sustain her life. One bottle was used, then two, three, and so on up to six, but no end to the bleeding was noticed.

The surgical team thought of calling in a senior doctor from a nearby city, but none was available. As a last measure they called in a young doctor from the local area. He came and saw that the bleeding was coming from a different spot than the other doctors were treating. To the great relief of the attending doctors the bleeding ultimately stopped. The patient regained consciousness after some time, but the proposed operation for her ailment had to be dropped.

Later, my nephew Dr. Gandhi treated Mrs. Kaur non-surgically for her hyperthyroid condition. The treatment was successful, and Mrs. Kaur started gaining weight. Eventually she recovered fully.

One day when she was at his office, she told Dr. Gandhi what had transpired during the operation. She said she was looking at the entire operation from outside her body. She related exactly what happened. My nephew was very skeptical and did not believe her at first. So he decided to test her veracity by asking for the names and descriptions of the doctors who were present. To his utter surprise she sputtered out all the names.

Still having some lurking doubts, he decided to test her further. Dr. Gandhi had not seen the doctor who had been called last and on whose diagnosis she ultimately recovered. He arranged to call all the doctors a few days later and asked her to identify each of them by name. She did it! My nephew was sure that she could not have learned their names except from the conversations in the operating theater that occurred when she was apparently unconscious.

I, too, would not have believed this incident had it not been narrated by my nephew whom I have no reason to doubt, and who in turn has nothing to gain from this story.

This incident called to my mind the concept, so succinctly exposed in the Hindu scripture, of the human soul being quite separate from the body. Perhaps in no other religion has this distinction of the mind or soul and the body been so clearly set out as in Hinduism. It is not our eyes that see, not our ears that hear, not our nose that smells, and not our brain that thinks. There is no way we can identify ourselves as anything other than the body we are encased in, except when we come across such unusual experiences.

The literature on extrasensory experiences is littered with countless incidents of how the spirit and the body are different. Here, however, is an example, empirically verified, which ought to boost our faith in religion, and the truth which is found in almost all religions, not excluding Christianity and Islam. It should prompt us to prefer good over evil, just over unjust in our daily lives, though we may all identify ourselves with our bodies during our temporary stay in the physical world without realizing its separateness from our real selves.

—*Sudhir Mehta,*
Hauppage, N.Y.

Out of Body, Out of Mind

What may be the most bizarre experience I ever had happened in 1972. It all began on a hot June morning when a frantic phone call from a doctor in St. Petersburg, Florida, changed the plans I had for the summer. Some surgery was planned for my mother. The doctor said she would not allow the surgery to be performed unless my wife and I were present.

As a teacher who looked forward to a summer of taking pictures for travel magazines, I was not too pleased with this change of plans. We prepared for the trip from western Michigan with a stop along the way at Marietta, Ohio, where my daughter and her family had moved. The visit with my daughter was not eventful, so we decided to stay at a hotel in downtown Marietta for the night.

We retired just before midnight. There was just enough light in the two-room suite for us to use the bathroom without bumping into any furniture. We were very tired and fell asleep almost immediately.

Shortly before one o'clock, I found myself wide awake. Instead of seeing the ceiling as if I were lying in bed, I saw a view of the bed from across the room about a dozen feet away. My wife was on the left side of the bed as usual. A middle-aged lady I had never seen before was standing next to the right side. I had no idea who she was or why she was standing there. It was much too early for room service.

She had gray hair combed straight back and oval glasses with gold rims. Her white dress had a distinctive pattern that reminded me of bamboo. She was there just long enough for me to remember what she looked like. As soon as I made an effort to remember details, she disappeared. I went back to sleep.

In the morning, I awoke on the right side of the bed. I puzzled over this mystery, trying to remember if I had ever read about two simultaneous out-of-body experiences while one of them is time-traveling. This happened years ago, and I have never heard or read about such an experience since.

At breakfast, I told my wife about this strange happening. I described every detail I could remember. We agreed on one thing: The woman was no one we ever saw before, or knew about.

It was a long drive to St. Petersburg. We arrived at the mobile home park where my mother lived. Since she was already in the hospital, she had made arrangements with her next-door neighbors to unlock the trailer so we could shower after our trip.

Jerry and Marion had anticipated our arrival. They had lunch prepared so we could go to the hospital later. Jerry, my wife, and I sat at the dining room table while Marion moved from the table to the kitchen carrying sandwiches and drinks. Marion stood at my right, and I carefully observed my wife across the table. Her eyes got bigger and bigger as she studied Marion. I was barely able to keep a straight face as I watched her look with stunned amazement at the unsuspecting Marion.

Marion was about five-foot four, with straight gray hair done up in a bun, wearing gold-rimmed glasses with oval lenses. The white dress was definitely a bamboo-leaf design.

I studied every book and article about out-of-body experiences I could find after this happened. There is no logical reason why Marion appeared to me a thousand miles away. She did not know what we looked like or where we were. She did not relay any message about the surgery. Neither did she leave any message at all. She never met us before. I doubt if Marion ever knew that an image of her appeared miles away in a hotel she never knew we stayed in. She had never seen us before. If the bedside image did not look exactly like Marion, I would have forgotten the incident entirely. I would have guessed that she was the image of a guest who died in the room we stayed in.

Now for the most perplexing part of the mystery. Why did I see Marion as if I were standing across the room? This may indicate we were both having an out-of-body experience at the same time. She did not relate or speak any message that would be a reason to time-travel a thousand miles away at one o'clock in the morning. She appeared for a very short time, just long enough for me to get a close enough look to grasp such details as age, size, and dress and to remember them accurately. There is no question in my mind that the real Marion looked exactly as I had described her to my wife.

We visited Marion and Jerry many times in the years that followed. We became good friends. In all of the conversations that followed, there never was a hint that Marion had time-traveled in her sleep before or since.

I am quite confident about what had transpired, but I don't understand many of the other mysteries we learn about.

—*Dominic P. Sondy,*
North Muskegon, Mich.

A Fever Pitched

I had my first and only out-of-body, near-death experience at five years of age, 79 years ago. At that time there were no antibiotics and few hospitals, and no 911 to call. Doctors made house calls only.

Both my ears were severely abscessed, and I had a raging fever of 105 degrees. Parents tried to heal their children with home remedies. I recall my mother, Viola Laris, and my grandmother, Bessie Dedes, dripping warm olive oil into my ears, alternating with heated towels that they held over a gas stove. I recall sitting up in bed, holding both hands over my ears, shaking my head from side to side with pain and screaming for hours.

I reached a point thereafter where I suddenly fell back on my pillow in a semi-stupor, which I believe put me in shock and near death. We had a holy icon of Jesus hanging on our wall across the room. As I lay weak and dazed, I riveted my half-closed eyes on the figure of Jesus. Suddenly I found myself slowly floating out of my body and crossing the room, still staring at the holy picture. I looked back at the figure lying on the bed. I knew it was me, but I wondered how I could be in two places at one time!

All at once Jesus began to emerge from the picture, growing taller as he descended toward me. I was mesmerized. I noticed the gold sandals he wore on his white, tapered feet as he came closer. In his arms he held layers of exquisitely colored cloth—the colors difficult to describe, just very vivid.

I held out my arms. He gently placed his in mine and said these words: "Give these to your mother and tell her to make clothes for you." He smiled, blessed me, and disappeared back into the picture!

I ran toward the kitchen to tell Mother. The moment I called out, I tripped over a small step, turned around, and quickly ran toward my bed, where I got right back into my body. At that moment, I bolted straight up in bed, with sweat pouring down my face, and screamed: "My pain is gone!"

I shall never forget how good I felt. I could feel the energy going through me. I jumped up and down and kept repeating, "Mama, I feel so good. Jesus came and gave me clothes!"

My mother and grandmother came in and touched my forehead.

"Her fever's gone—how could that be?" they wondered. They were in tears, and crossing themselves in amazement. I kept pointing to the picture of Jesus, and my mother said slowly: "You know, this child was healed by a higher power."

I know now that I had been moments away from death. Jesus (who I think is an Adept) shot energy through me, and brought me back to life. It was obvious that I had a major healing.

—*Ethel Rawson,*
Harwood Heights, Ill.

To the Brink and Back

I was born in January 1920, and I have had three near-death experiences. The first happened when I had measles at age seven. We had gone on a trip to Leadville, Colorado, a town above the timberline in the mountains southwest of Denver. My father worked in road construction all over the state of Colorado and he was going up there to check out a job.

We traveled in a Model-T dump truck. It was early fall, and it was getting cold. Three of us kids were on a feather bed covered with quilts in the back of the truck. My baby sister was wrapped in blankets on my mother's lap on the front seat. There was not a cab on that truck.

We stayed in a hotel overnight in Leadville, and it was so cold in that room. It had linoleum on the floor that felt like ice when you walked barefoot on it.

On our way home, I was in the back of the truck again. I thought I was going to freeze to death. By the time we got home to Englewood (just south of Denver), I was running a high fever and had red spots all over me.

I was lying in bed, so sick, when all of a sudden I found myself up in the clouds. I knew I was on my way to Heaven, and I began to cry, thinking that my mother would be sad because I was gone. At that, I snapped back into my body. I was still terribly sick, but I lived through it.

The second experience occurred when I was 22 years old and mother of a 15-month-old boy. I was home in bed, sick with pneumonia. Suddenly, I found myself going through a tunnel of light. When I got to the end of the tunnel I stepped into the golden light that surrounded me with such love. I felt so good, and I wanted to stay. I could see people in the distance waving to me. But then the thought of my little boy came into my mind, and wham! I was back into my body.

From that pneumonia I developed tuberculosis and entered a sanitarium in Denver. There was no medication for TB at that time. You had to stay in the bed all the time. You weren't even allowed out of your bed to go to the restroom; you had to use a bedpan. (Yuck!)

At the sanitarium, my right lung was collapsed through a procedure known as pneumothorax. The doctor would insert a long needle between the ribs, like a valve in a tire, and pump air into the pleural cavity. This would collapse the lung and help it to heal. It was very much like putting a splint on a very badly cut knuckle to keep it immobile. This procedure was done many times a week for four years; by the fifth year, it was only once a week.

When the doctor first began this treatment I had my third near-death experience. I left my body and went through the tunnel of light. When I stepped into the golden light, I thought, Oh boy! I'm here at last! But there was a gentleman standing just inside the light. He smiled, shook his head, and wham! I was back here again. I'm sure it was Jesus.

—*Ava Belle Chucta,*
Crossnore, N.C.

Haunted Places

Sometimes the collective can end up believing in a paradox. In 2005, Gallup reported that 32 percent of people believed in ghosts—that the "spirits of dead people can come back in certain places/situations"—while 37 percent believed "that houses can be haunted."

Interesting how 5 percent of respondents could believe in haunted houses without believing in ghosts! Either this illustrates that (a) some people believe haunted houses can be occupied by some entity other than a ghost, (b) that the people taking the poll didn't quite understand the nature of the questions being asked, or (c) people have contradictory beliefs.

While I would give them the benefit of the doubt—agreeing that not all haunted places are necessarily occupied by ghosts, i.e., the spirit of a once-living human versus, say, a demonic entity or otherworldly beast—the persistence of confusion inevitably disturbs our credibility.

So here are some of the facts. A haunting generally occurs in one of two ways. Either the haunting can be residual in nature, or it can be intelligent. In the case of a residual haunting, a sort of playback loop is created at some point, where an intense amount of emotion was felt by the spirit now "trapped" at the location. These entities usually repeat a single act over and over again, with no regard for the living. In the case of an intelligent haunting, the spirit is still very much aware of their current surroundings and actually attempts to interact with the living.

This is precisely why we offer these stories—to clear up the confusion that has so obfuscated the truth and altered the credibility of this burgeoning, yet priceless category of, what we consider paranormal scientific inquiry. Here are some of those places, things, and energies that have called out for recognition, begging at least for consideration in the sea of misinformation.

The Haunted House

Nestled in the wooded hills just south of Mishawaka, Indiana, stands a beautiful two-story home. It was once owned by the parents of my best friend, Pam Krizman. Pam had one of the two bedrooms upstairs, and her cousin Robbie (Roberta Banach) had the other.

One night while Pam was sleeping, she thought she heard a rustling sound coming from her closet. Moonlight was shining through the window, so she was able to see fairly well in the dark. She looked over to where she heard the noise, and as her eyes adjusted to the light she saw what looked like a tall, dark shadow moving across her room. It made a rasping sound as if it were someone having trouble breathing. As she watched, it floated through her closed door. She was terrified, and like most kids who get scared, she pulled the covers up over her head. After a while she fell asleep.

The next morning when she awoke, Pam decided not to say anything to the rest of the family because she thought no one would believe her. She went downstairs to breakfast. A few minutes later, Robbie came and sat at the table. Pam could hardly believe it when Robbie started talking about seeing a black figure floating through her room and making a sound like someone having trouble breathing. When Pam told her the same thing had happened in her room, they knew they had both seen the same ghost.

Pam's mom told her the previous owner of the house was an elderly woman who had passed away in the bedroom that was now Pam's. The woman had severe asthma and had a hard time breathing. So now they knew who their ghostly visitor was.

This was not the only time the ghost made its presence known. One night, Pam's brother Art and some of his football buddies came to the house after a game. The rest of the family was out for the evening, so the house was empty. As Art walked upstairs and into the hallway, there was a mist-like fog in the middle of the hall right next to Pam's bedroom door. When Art and his buddies saw it, they ran down the stairs and left a note for his mom and dad that said, "I'm staying over at my friend's for the night—the house is acting up again!"

This all happened back in the 1960s. Many times I have driven past the house and wondered if the new owners ever had any ghostly happenings. I've been tempted to knock on their door and tell them they live in a haunted house. But, then again, maybe it's just as well I don't. Some things are best left alone.

—*Fran Frisk Lenyo,*
Mishawaka, Ind.

South Minneapolis

In an old south Minneapolis district called "the Hub of Hell," there was once a row of clapboard houses wedged between the tracks and the train barns. They were small, sooty houses with white-lace curtains, wooden walks, and picket fences with sagging gates. The warped porches showed signs of wear from the rough-and-tumble play of children, the harsh winters, and the scraping of chairs where renters escaped the hot, muggy nights after a day of toil.

This is where my grandparents lived and reared their three sons and one daughter after they had emigrated from Germany through Ellis Island in 1899. One son, Otto, became a streetcar conductor, married, and moved three blocks east toward the Mississippi River. Another son, Fritz, worked at the foundry beside his father. At age 14, my mother, Frieda, worked in a candy factory. She and Grandmother often waited up for the youngest son, Julius, who had become a brakeman, riding on the top of the trains, on the Milwaukee Road.

They were on the porch this particular sticky, windless night in August 1914. It was nearly bedtime when they heard a clatter through the open windows. Thinking the cat was in the cupboards, they hurried inside. The cat was arched, with fur standing on end, the dishes were slightly askew, and the pendulum clock stopped at 9:55. Julius had visited. He would not be coming home again.

—*Holly M. Collett,*
Tucson, Ariz.

An Old Country House

People who are born with a "veil" over their face are often sensitive to phenomena that elude the rest of us. My mother, Eva King, was such a person. I know she possessed psychic sensitivity to some degree. I was present when she apprehended—someway, somehow, without knowledge through normal cognitive channels—the sudden and unexpected death of her father.

I had heard her speak of other unusual experiences. One that particularly intrigued me concerned what in all likelihood was a haunted house that she, my father, and older brother and sister occupied many years before I was born. Here is the way she told it to me:

"Some people don't believe in ghosts. Neither did your father when we first moved into the old farmhouse in Monroe County, West Virginia. It was a quiet, lovely place. The house was made of logs, and was comfortable enough. It was really a nice place to live. Or so we thought when we first moved in! For things started happening soon afterward that changed our minds—eerie, frightening things. Your father was unaware of them at first, but he too decided later that the place was strange and unwholesome.

"One evening, your brother and sister and I were sitting in the yard near the front porch. We were cracking hickory nuts on a large, flat rock. Your father was away at work. Suddenly, all three of us heard voices coming from an upstairs room in the house. I knew no one was in the house, yet the voices were plainly audible. There were two, a man's and a woman's.

"Another time we heard an alarm clock ringing upstairs. I knew we had put no alarm clock in any of the rooms up there, which we did not occupy, but I went up to investigate. Sure enough, no clock was found. But the ringing had been just as clear as those unexplained voices conversing.

"Like many such houses, the cellar was reached by steps leading down from the porch. There was a peculiar sound associated with the cellar that both disturbed and puzzled us. It was the sound of someone pulling a big box down the steps to the cellar. We would go and look—no box, nobody! This occurred several times.

"Then we started seeing things as well. What it was that the children and I saw one warm dark evening I'll never know. We were playing 'bear,' and I was the bear. We ran back and forth over the yard, and around the house, having a lot of fun. The children would squeal with fright when I growled and chased them. The front porch was long, as was the custom with such old farmhouses. As the dusk grew deeper, I saw something move down at the far end of the porch. For the life of me, it looked just like a great black bear. Whatever it was, the thing raised up and put its front paws on the porch. Something had decided to play 'bear' with us!

"Scared half out of our wits, the children and I ran inside, through the back door. We fastened all the windows and doors. We heard nothing those long hours that we cowered inside, waiting for your father to come home. Eventually, he did. There was never any sign of a bear, nor did anyone ever see such an animal in that vicinity. I often wondered what the thing had been, and if we had been playing 'wolf' instead of 'bear,' would it have assumed a different shape?

"Then something happened to your brother one night that really gave me a fright. He was sleeping at the foot of the bed. Suddenly, he called out that something was on him, mashing him. He couldn't breathe. I got up and turned on the light. He was crying, badly frightened, and gasping for breath. I let him sleep next to me the rest of the night. And I left the light burning.

"This could have been explained away as a nightmare, or a child's imagination, had it not been for all the other unusual happenings.

"We should have moved away then, but we stayed on. Houses and jobs weren't easy to find.

"The strange happenings continued. Your father and I had gathered a lot of apples. We intended to peel them and make apple butter. We piled the apples in one of the far vacant rooms. It was a big house, and we only used part of it. One cloudy, lonely day we decided to make the apple butter—or at least begin peeling the apples. I went to the room for a load of apples to take up to the kitchen. As I went out of the room, it seemed as if someone was walking behind me. It gave me a creepy sensation. I made three trips for apples, and each time there was the same feeling. It made me shaky. I told your father. He scoffed at me, and said there was nothing to fear, just my nerves.

"'I'm not going back in that room for any more apples,' I said. 'If you want more, you'll have to get them yourself.'

"He did. When he returned, he had a curious expression on his face. 'You were right,' he said. 'I got the same feeling. Exactly as if there was someone walking behind me!' We knew then for certain that more than our imaginations was involved. All of us, including the children, were aware of the disturbing influences in that old country farmhouse.

"Considering the history of the old house, there was good reason for it to be haunted. We found out later that one former resident had jumped from the portico and killed himself, another had died suddenly in his chair, and a third had hanged himself in the barn. Perhaps something had driven them to such measures. I don't know. I only knew that we had had enough.

"We moved. The next house we lived in did not have such sounds and sensations."

—*Herman Stowell King,*
Wicomico, Va.

Bloody Handprint

My mother died in 1965 of lung cancer. About a year later, my father died of a heart attack. A month or so after my father's death, a neighbor came through the back door for a visit. She asked me who the man in the bedroom was. But there was no one in the bedroom.

Several times while leaving or arriving at the house, a large man's figure was seen moving in front of the window. Searches of the house were relentless, but there was no man in the house.

Then one night, I was going up the front steps of the house with my fiancée when we heard a loud slapping sound. My fiancée screamed, and there was a large, bloody handprint on her arm. But there was no one there.

Shortly after the bloody handprint incident, I was drafted and the house was sold while I was in the army. I never returned to the house—and I never will.

—*Warren Brewer,*
Bremen, Ga.

Blue Aura Ghost

Still to this day I have not forgotten what I call the "Blue Aura Ghost."

When I was about seven or eight, my mother had enrolled me at a day care, which is no longer in existence. I went to kindergarten there. They had a system for grade-school children: If the parents had to work early, they could drop off the children; then a bus would come and take the children to school. Later, the bus would take the children back to the day care, where their parents would pick them up.

An elderly lady we fondly called "Grandma." The ran the day care. There was a rumor that Grandma's late husband haunted the houses along the block on which the day care was located.

One day, my friends decided they wanted to go on a "ghost hunt." We were upstairs in the music room, which had a TV we could watch until it was time for school so we didn't have to be with the younger kids. I was not interested; I didn't believe in the ghost, but being seven or eight I was kind of spooked.

I sat and watched TV while they did their ghost hunt. Then we heard, "School bus is here!" Everyone rushed out, leaving me to pick up. I looked back behind me to protest when I saw a figure . . . it was an old man, dressed in a white robe with a hood, standing in the doorway, and he had a blue aura around him. He looked sort of malevolent, yet I knew he was not. I just stared, then looked away, then looked back to see he was gone.

Some years later I met up with one of "Grandma's" granddaughters when we were in high school. We were talking and I told her of my experience. She said her family had also had some strange experiences, and they believe it to be their grandfather.

I wonder, if that was "him" that I saw, why did he choose me to show himself?

—*Janis Cramlett,*
Rockford, Ill.

Magnanimous Maude

You may wonder why such a label as "Magnanimous Maude" would be attached to an apparition. It is because she proved to be my best friend in a small, unfriendly town situated in northern Minnesota. Maude was kind. She was generous in her heart. She allowed an attachment that is virtually unknown in this mix of real and spirit world. I have hesitated to write about her because of the special quality of our relatively short, but intense, relationship.

It was 1959. Because I had three young children to consider, I had not yet decided upon a position since June graduation from the University of Minnesota. Well, it had to be done. I decided not to move too far away from my parents, who had become a mainstay in our lives since our abandonment. There was a job open in the schools north of Minneapolis, which would be a relatively short two-hour drive on the weekend for Dad or myself.

Priding myself in generally being able to handle the unknown and make friends easily, I decided to look into it. Living in a small town appealed to me greatly.

Not only would it be restful but my two younger children, who were boys, would be less apt to find trouble. My daughter would also have the opportunity for growth without the need to constantly monitor her brothers.

After a few inquiries, I found the only rental available. It was a lovely old place with a turret, stained glass windows, a wide wraparound porch, and a curved staircase. The entrance hall would easily accommodate all those wet boots and heavy winter clothing, and the stairway, hallway, and front rooms were nicely situated. It was a 14-room, typical, unaltered Victorian home. It was set back on the lot with a grand front yard and a field behind it. The elementary school was one and a half blocks away.

My dad moved us in lock, stock, and barrel. He had saved a lot of near-antique furniture, and with all the hardwood floors and lovely mahogany woodwork, we were content. Each child had a private room. The potbellied stove in the kitchen took away the chill. The oil furnace worked.

I found out shortly that there wasn't much to do without a movie or drama group in town; however, that was fine. I started to read the books I had never had time to pursue after the children's bedtime stories. My evenings were cozy, wrapped in a quilt in one of the rockers.

My first intimation that I was not alone was when I noticed the rocker beside me rocking gently of its own volition. I recall thinking *Isn't this nice? I have company in this cold, old town where people have not wanted my friendship.* And I let it go at that.

Then my older son started waking up because the hanging lightbulb above his bed was on. He was seven. I began to check on this phenomenon and would turn it off and return downstairs to my activity.

Sometimes I felt the swishing of a long, silken skirt beside me on the staircase, and I would say, "Come along, whoever you are, and we will sit awhile."

Along about holiday time, a teenage neighbor boy said to me, "You know the house you live in is haunted, don't you?" He is the one who told me my friend's name was Maude. She had a last name too. Altogether her name was old-fashioned and quite lovely.

It was good to know what to call her. Now when the light went on above my child's bed, I asked, "Please don't turn the light on, Maude." After two requests—the second with an explanation—the lighting stopped.

Maude seemed content with my residing in her home and with my friendship. Occasionally something would be moved from its place and often she was beside me on the staircase. It was comforting to have a congenial companion in this cold, old town.

I was offered a position the following year at the Minneapolis Hearing Society. Before I left the manse

I said a reluctant and appreciative goodbye to Maude, the very fine lady of the house.

—*Holly M. Collett,*
Tucson, Ariz.

My Grandparents' House

My mother's parents, Mr. and Mrs. Frederick Ingwersen, built a house in about 1896 at 4105 Stuart Street in North Denver, Colorado. It was a two-story red brick building with a large front portico and an enclosed back porch. The second floor was large enough for an apartment, but was left vacant for many years. The access to the upper floor was from the kitchen on the first floor via a stairway that had a landing in the middle. On the far end of the second floor, there was another stairway going down to a vestibule by the front door. The house had a very small fruit and vegetable cellar. On one end, there were shelves for home-canned goods. These were covered with a bedsheet to keep dust from them.

One night in about 1902, when my mother, Marie, was a teenager, she was in the dining room with her family on the first floor. They heard a marble rolling across the floor above them. It rolled to the top of the back stairs, then dropped down the steps one at a time. It rolled across the landing and continued to bounce down the steps until it hit the closed door at the bottom of the stairway. When the door was opened, there was no marble. This event happened many times and no marble was ever found.

One time when we were visiting our grandparents, my grandmother asked my teenage sister Bertha to go down to the cellar to get some canned fruit. When she approached the shelf, the form of a person became visible behind the sheet that hung in front of the shelves. It moved forward a little ways, and the sheet was tight around the whole body. Bertha was almost scared to death and ran up the stairs.

Grandmother wouldn't believe what happened. She said the wind moved the sheet—even though there was no source for the wind. Bertha never went into that cellar again.

About 1930, we visited my grandparents and I was bored being with the adults, so I asked if I could go upstairs to play some games. My mother said I could, but she told me not to go on the front stairway. She said there was something very bad there.

I went up and played awhile, but being seven years old I just had to see what was bad about the front stairs. I took a few steps down. I saw nothing, but I froze with fear. I couldn't move; I screamed and cried hysterically until my mother came and carried me down to the front room. After I quit crying, she said, "I told you not to go on those stairs. We all know there is something bad up there."

About 1941, when I was a teenager, my parents and I had a discussion about the strange and frightening events that happened in the old house. I asked them if they knew of anything that happened in the house, such as a murder or death that could have caused these things. My mother said that her parents built the house, and she knew of no event that was bad or unusual. My father said he lived near that area when he was a boy, and he and some friends played near the location of the house. One day they found a rusted revolver, and at that time they thought a battle had taken place there many years before.

We came to the conclusion that someone being murdered or killed in battle at the location of the old house could have caused it to be haunted.

—*Stanley R. Colson,*
Indian Harbor Beach, Fla.

No Feet

I do not understand why a person like me, who is afraid of her own shadow, likes so much to write about the unknown. When I started writing the tale of "No Feet," I had to do it in the daytime, because at night all the hairs of my arms would stand up and I could not move my hand to write.

This is the story of what happened to me and my dear friend Aurora in 1979, over in Rio Piedras, Puerto

Rico, where we both were living. Aurora was waiting that morning for Panchito, a man who was going to divide her parlor with plywood panels. She was a widow, and her sons were married and lived in different places around town. The oldest (Victor) wanted to be near her to help with all the problems of being a widow. He came up with the idea to divide the parlor. That part of the house had two entrances. Once the panels were put in, it would become a cozy little apartment for his mother, and the rest of the house would be perfect for Victor and his family. Victor had a close friend, Panchito, with knowledge of carpentry.

All this could only be done now that Aurora's husband had died. He had never allowed her to put a nail in the walls while he was alive. Now she was sure that her dead husband would not mind, but it had been very difficult for the kids to make her change her mind. For the past two years, she had been living with her dead husband's spirit. The whole house was suspended in time, surrounded with wrought iron gates all around and an enclosed driveway, giving you the impression of a catacomb. She had kept the house just the way it was when her husband died—all the ashtrays were full of his stained cigarette butts, and the print of his head still remained on his pillow.

Being alone made it easy for her to think her husband was still there with her. She talked to him, and—believe it or not—he responded. We all felt his presence through the uneasiness that hearing her talk caused us.

One night my husband and I gave Aurora a ride home. As my husband took the key of the gate to open it, he felt a strong chill and returned the key to Aurora.

"Please take the key; this place gives me the creeps," he said.

"That's nothing, dear," I told him. "Wait until we get inside. It's like entering a catacomb—fear surrounds you and will try to suffocate you."

Unaware of my comment, Aurora looked inside, smiling, and said, "Surprise! Look who brought me home, dear."

We did not stay long, leaving Aurora with her memories and the company of her beloved dead husband.

Next morning Panchito arrived and she welcomed him with a smile. "How good of you to come so early, I really would like you to finish this tonight."

Panchito said, "Doña Aurora, to tell you the truth, I would never dare to set a foot in this house at night; people are telling me things. . ."

Aurora smiled. "Nonsense—pay no attention to gossips; just tell me how much are you going to charge me."

Panchito smiled back and said, "Doña, for you, nada—just a cup of coffee and a sandwich will do."

She said, "I am out of coffee, but I'll go to the corner store and get what I need. I'll be back soon; inside you will find all you need for the job."

Panchito got down on his knees next to the tools and the rest of the materials, whistling a popular tune. With measuring tape in hand, he started to measure. But then a very cold air wrapped him up and he started to tremble. A heavy and unknown force prevented him from moving. Out of the corner of his eye he saw a pair of pants standing very close to him. He tried to figure out how a pair of pants could stand so straight, when there were no feet supporting them!

Panchito began to sweat. He tried to get up, but all was in vain. He felt sick and sensed goosebumps all over his body. That is when he decided to crawl. He had to get away from that thing that was about to catch up to him. As he crawled, the pants followed him as fast as they could! He got to the driveway, opened the gate, and ran to his car and got in. That's where Aurora found him, white as chalk. He never entered the house again.

Victor had to put up the wall. The neighborhood found out what happened to Panchito and no one dared to go to that house ever again.

Father John, from their church, came to the house a couple of times and begged Aurora to get rid of all the belongings of her dead husband.

After that, Aurora and I used to meet at my house. I swore I would never go back to her house as long as I lived. I did not want to meet "No Feet!"

—Helen Torres,
Christmas, Fla.

Secret of the Closet

It was a raw, chilly day in March when Mother and Dad moved into the new home they had just bought in the northwest side of Chicago. It was an "income" home with three flats. Dad wanted the first floor apartment. The basement and upper floor were rented out.

Immediately my two daughters, Janine (age three) and Bonnie (age six), asked to stay overnight with Gram and Grandpa. They agreed to have the girls come in about a month, which would give Grandma time to get all settled. The girls looked forward to sleeping in the new house and eating Gram's delicious plum cakes.

The month passed quickly, and soon the girls were packing their pajamas to stay with Gram and Grandpa in their brand new house. One would think they were planning a trip to Europe! I left the girls in Grandma's capable hands.

The next evening when I went to pick them up, they had a strange story to tell me. They said that after Grandma tucked them in and left after the night prayers a strange thing occurred. The figure of a man emerged from the closet and stood at the foot of their bed staring at them. They were so frightened they pulled the blankets over their heads and fell asleep after a while.

At first I thought the girls were spinning a tale, so I asked Grandma about it. She had a tale just as strange! Her story was that whenever she left that closet door open, strange vibrations filled the room, and one night when she left the door open a dark figure emerged from it and stood at the foot of her bed. She turned on the bed lamp and the figure disappeared.

Evidently Grandma had forgotten to close the closet door when she bedded down the girls. My thoughts were, "There is a troubled spirit asking for help."

I was able to obtain the address of the former owner of the house—a widow. She was living in the Chicago suburb of Skokie with her daughter. After locating the house I was introduced to Mrs. Hans Schmidt. She was friendly and spoke with an accent.

Mrs. Schmidt said she sold the home because of some bad memories. Here is the story, as she told it to me:

"My husband Hans had borrowed some money from his brother to buy the house. His brother bargained with him after a while to stay with us, using the balance of the money owed him to cover his room and board. However, Hans disagreed and an argument ensued. Hans pushed his brother aside, as he thought he was going to strike him. His brother fell backwards, striking his head on a rock by the garden gate. He died instantly.

"After that Hans became despondent and would sit for hours at a time in the bedroom, just staring into space.

"One afternoon I went shopping and when I came home, I found Hans hanging by one of my clotheslines in the closet. He just couldn't forgive himself for the death of his brother and so he hanged himself. His spirit still occupies the closet and I was afraid I didn't know how to handle it, so I sold the house."

I then told Mrs. Schmidt I would go to the rectory and make arrangements for the priest to come and perform some rituals to give Hans' spirit peace. Mrs. Schmidt and all her family attended the rituals. We all prayed for the soul's release and set the spirit free to enjoy everlasting peace.

After the rituals we found no vibrations in the room when the closet door was left open. No one walked from the closet to the bed at night—it was so peaceful. Hans' spirit was set free.

—*Lillian Burton,*
River Grove, Ill.

Spirits Among Us

In the fall of 1983 we were living in southwest Houston when my ten-year-old son began telling me, "There are spirits in this house, especially in my room."

At first he didn't seem too upset about the fact that we might be sharing our space with disembodied people. But as the weeks passed, he became ever more agitated. He was especially afraid to go to sleep at night. I explained how to bring the protective Light into his body. Still, he was frightened and would only go to bed with his Bible clutched firmly against his chest.

Without telling him, fearing that it might encourage this possible "flight of the imagination" yet fully aware of the possibility of spirits sharing our space, I began to regularly purge the entire house with the Light.

During this time my son also told me about a bedroom in the house of his little friend who lived across the street. He said that their dog, which normally followed them everywhere, refused to go with them when they played in one particular room. Apparently, even when they picked the dog up and carried him into the room, he would shiver and quake, waiting for the first opportunity to escape.

One night in early November the little boy across the street slept over, and I dreamed the kids and I had visitors. There was a girl of about 12 with frizzy red hair who was head-and-shoulders taller than my son, along with her parents. All were dressed in farmer-type clothes. The females wore dark print dresses with gathered skirts.

The girl was being a brat while her parents stood by and said nothing to her. Since they were "guests," I hesitated to say or do anything. Then I walked into my son's room and saw this girl throw him onto the bed, jump on top of him, and sock him in the eye while her dad stood silently right behind her. I erupted. I grabbed the girl by the hair and pulled her off my son. She began fighting me, trying to throw me down, but my feet felt as if they were bolted to the floor.

When I awoke I immediately recorded the dream in my dream diary. At breakfast two wide-eyed boys began telling me about their nocturnal visitors. I was amazed when they described the same people I had seen in my dream. It was time for me to reconsider my previous position and accept the possibility that we did indeed have spirits in the house and that these kids could see them, although I could not.

All that day I pondered the possibilities. It was obvious that these ghosts were not friendly. Perhaps they felt that we were intruding on their space. It struck me as strange that a small area of the house across the street also seemed to be haunted. I couldn't help but wonder how many of my other neighbors' houses might also be so occupied. Frequently during the day I went into my son's room to see if I could pick up any vibrations. I couldn't.

That evening I went into my son's bedroom and said, "I've been thinking about your ghosts." He stared at me wide-eyed as I continued. "I can't help but think that they might have all been killed suddenly, maybe in an Indian raid or perhaps overrun by Santa Ana's army as they marched from San Antonio to San Jacinto. We're right in line for that. Anyway, I wonder if they might have been killed so suddenly that they really don't realize that they're dead. It could be that they had a cabin on this spot and they feel that we are the intruders."

"I s'pose," he answered, then a worried frown creased his forehead. "But how can we get them to leave?"

I shrugged. "I guess we could try sending them to the Light, like in the Poltergeist movies."

His face brightened. "Let's try it!"

"Are they here now?"

He looked slowly around the room, then back at me. He nodded his head toward the opposite end of the room. "Over there in the corner by the bathroom."

Slowly, I walked toward the spot he had indicated. Sure enough, as I approached the corner I could feel a sudden chill in the air. I shivered. Would these beings turn on us if we tried to communicate with them? How should we go about it? The only thing I was sure of was that we had to protect ourselves with the Light before we tried to do anything.

I returned to the bed, sat down beside my son, and took his hand. "The first thing we have to do is bring in the Light," I told him. "Close your eyes and let's both concentrate."

He nodded and closed his eyes. I did the same and began to visualize the guarding beam flooding into our bodies. When I felt that we were both glowing strongly I murmured, "Okay, now I guess we try to communicate telepathically. First, try to get their attention. Then we can tell them that they no longer belong on this plane and that they need to move on. Direct them to go toward the Light."

For several long moments we concentrated deeply. When I felt that we were indeed making contact, I proceeded with the rest of my planned message. After several more minutes of mentally repeating the instructions, I felt as if our mission might have been accomplished. Slowly I opened my eyes.

"Okay," I said. "Look around and tell me what you see."

My son opened his eyes and searched every nook and cranny of the room. He turned toward me with a broad grin on his face. "They're not here! They're gone. We did it!"

I walked slowly around the room. There was not a chilly spot anywhere. The spirits apparently had gone and they never returned.

—Dottie Goudy,
Houston, Tex.

The Haunting of Effie Street

I had spoken to Laura Fong only briefly on two previous occasions. Therefore, I was more than a little surprised when Steve Harper, a mutual friend, rang me up to inquire if he could arrange an informal meeting. He made it clear it would not be a social call, but would say little more. I was intrigued by the notion and readily agreed.

At the appointed time, Steve made the introductions and I escorted the two of them to my study, where we settled in to discuss the nature of their visit.

Steve had conveyed to Laura that I was a writer and an investigator of paranormal activity. "Laura feels there is some sort of manifestation in her home."

In serious tones, Laura asked me if I would consider looking into it.

I studied the young woman's face for a moment and could read nothing but unrestrained fear. Of course, I agreed to help. A day was chosen to initiate the investigation, and we parted.

I arrived at her home at five o'clock on the appointed day. The house was located in a radically deteriorated neighborhood in the old downtown core of the city. The house itself was large and ancient, built prior to electricity and indoor plumbing. Both utilities were added at a much later date. The house must have been a showplace before falling on hard times. A covered wooden porch, so common in Victorian times, wrapped itself around the exterior. There was an exterior set of stairs to the upper floor that had been added when the house was divided into an upper and lower set of apartments.

On that foggy autumn evening, it was not a very inviting scene. But it was just what a girl putting herself through college on a limited income could afford. Laura lived in the lower unit.

The contrast with the exterior was striking. With a secondhand-store budget and a lot of elbow grease, she had made the lower unit very warm and cozy.

Laura offered me a glass of wine and told me she would have something for us to eat in about 45 minutes. Until then, I could make myself comfortable in the living room.

I pulled a magnifying glass from my duffel bag and began tracing along the baseboard and molding for any hidden wires. I could feel Laura's presence. I looked over my shoulder, and she had a puzzled expression on her face. "What are you doing?" she asked.

"I'm looking for wiring, hidden cavities in the walls, anything that looks like it doesn't belong." I explained that I had been a student of magic since childhood and that it was actually fairly easy to rig a good spook show. Laura laughed and went back into the kitchen. I found nothing out of the ordinary.

Next, I retrieved a spool of fine-gauge wire and a sack of flour from my duffel bag and went out onto the porch. I strung a zigzagging trip line from the house to the spokes of the railing, crisscrossing the walkway calf-high. Carefully avoiding the trip wires, I spread a thin coating of flour the length of the porch. As I was tossing the last of the flour, Laura came onto the porch calling me in to eat.

After our dinner, Laura put on a pot of coffee and we settled in the living room. I inquired why she stayed in the house. Wasn't it possible for her to get some financial assistance from her family? She hesitated for a moment, and then in a strong voice told me how greatly she valued her independence.

She asked me what I had been doing out on the porch. I explained that, according to the information she had provided, the likely path of the manifestation was along the porch. She nodded agreement, and I continued. "If anyone of an ordinary physical nature is causing these disturbances, I promise you the trip wires will snag him. Even if he's able to avoid those, it's impossible for his feet not to leave an impression in the flour."

As the evening grew late, Laura suggested we try to catch a few winks, as the specter rarely made an appearance before midnight. I unpacked my sleeping bag and rolled it out the length of the couch. Laura wished me pleasant dreams in her most ironic tone and closed her bedroom door.

A couple of hours later, I was startled into consciousness by a firm hand wrenching my shoulder.

"My God, don't you hear it? How could you sleep through it?"

I bolted into a sitting position, trying to clear my head and focus my eyes. I checked my watch—it was 12:27 a.m. There were muffled sounds coming from the floor above our heads.

"You can hear it much clearer in my room." There was a shadow of fear in Laura's voice.

I followed her into her room. Emanating from the ceiling above us were the distinct sounds of heavy feet shuffling across the floor.

"You're sure nobody lives upstairs?"

Laura could feel the tension in my voice. "No—when I moved in I asked my landlady about the upper unit. She said no one had lived there in years."

We stared into each other's faces as the shuffling continued. The footsteps developed a regimented pattern, crossing from one side of the room to the other, where a window faced the street. The pattern continued for approximately 20 minutes, then abruptly halted. The footfalls now moved toward the front door and the stairs. The room was growing perceptibly colder by the moment.

Laura's eyes were extremely wide, and her fear was now tangible. "He'll be coming down the stairs now. He always does."

"Do you know that it's a man?"

Laura looked a little confused as she considered the question. "You know, it's strange you ask that. Even though I've never seen him, I just get that impression." I nodded my understanding and then, as if on cue, we both heard the front door open and shut and methodical footsteps tumbling down the stairs. The slow heavy footsteps continued around the porch, as if passing effortlessly through the trip wires. A shadow, with the clear outline of a man, passed over Laura's window heading for her front door.

There was now steam coming from our lips and both our hearts had hitched up a notch or two. "You stay here, Laura. I'm going to follow it." She was too frightened to argue and nodded vigorously.

I stepped into the living room just as the shadow floated past the window. As it passed, the clomping sound of its feet ceased, leaving only an echo. Quickly, I grabbed my flashlight and flung open the door. Only a void greeted me, and the twisting tendrils of fog glistening in the glow of the streetlamp. It was impossible for anything of flesh and blood to have escaped my attention.

Stepping lightly onto the grass, I worked my way around the perimeter of the house. All of the tripwires were intact and none of the flour had been disturbed. Reaching the stairs cautiously, I mounted them. The front door had a hasp and sturdy padlock. Both were still firmly in force. Retracing my way down the steps, I began to work my way back to Laura's when I saw a bright light on in the upper unit; just as quickly it was extinguished.

Nothing further of any consequence happened that evening. Two days later, I dropped by to do a little background checking. I knocked for what seemed an eternity at the door of Laura's neighbor. Finally, an ancient Hispanic lady opened the door a mere sliver. I explained the occasion of my visit and she became a little friendlier. She spoke broken English and the wrinkles around her eyes crackled when she smiled.

I asked her if she had lived there long. She proudly replied, "For over 70 years." I asked if she had ever seen teenagers or vandals entering the unit. She didn't think it was possible, as it was her understanding the windows had been nailed shut and the door padlocked.

Finally—and most importantly—I inquired if anything strange or traumatic had occurred in the upper unit. She rolled her eyes and smiled with a knowing grin. Some 30 years prior an old man had lived in the upper unit. He was very lonely and unhappy. After some time his daughter, who lived out of state, made arrangements for him to come live with her. She was driving out to pick him up. However, for some reason, she was delayed and unable to contact him. The old lady remembered seeing him going up and down the stairs and walking back and forth to the window that looked down into the street. When the daughter finally arrived, her father had been dead two days.

"Probably a heart attack," I commented absently.

"More likely a broken heart," the old lady said wisely.

Back home, I began to pull together the pieces of the puzzle. I contacted Laura's landlady and informed her that someone was using the lights in the upper unit. She commented that it was quite impossible, as the power had been discontinued to that unit years ago.

The following day, I made my final trip to the house on Effie Street. Laura was in the process of moving. Plainly stated, her sanity was of more value than her independence.

—P.M. Hart,
Fresno, Calif.

The House Remembers

The house stands in an older Seattle neighborhood on a hill a couple of blocks above Lake Washington. It is a gracious house, well-kept, with a huge plum tree in the backyard, rockery in the front, and real leaded glass windows. It has a secret life.

The house belonged to my parents in 1960, when my husband and I and our three children drove up from California to visit, settling into the basement guest room.

The house must have had a long life and was most likely built for a large family, but at that time both my parents worked and the house was lonely.

It has been said that strong emotions can imprint themselves on the atmosphere of a place. Sometimes the activity will replay itself as though on a tape loop and those emotions will occur again and again.

The first time I was left alone in the house with my toddler, the house came to life. The rest of the family had gone out shopping. I was in the guest room folding laundry while my daughter napped.

It had been a couple of hours, so I wasn't surprised when everyone returned. I heard the front door open and much talk and laughter from both adults and children. I went upstairs to greet them—but the entry hall was empty.

I looked in the living room, dining room, and kitchen. I climbed the stairs to the bedrooms, but by then I knew I was alone.

Two days later my parents went to work, my husband took the two older kids to the lake, and the house replayed the tape again. This time I wasn't so surprised.

That evening I asked my mother when she had planned to tell me about the "problem" with the house. She admitted that she had hoped I wouldn't notice because she didn't want me to be afraid to be alone.

We decided that this gracious old home was replaying a particularly happy, exciting moment in its "memory" to lighten the long, quiet days.

—Sylvia Webb-Hutchins,
Bellingham, Wash.

What Was It? We Don't Talk About it!

A cousin who died a couple of years ago once told me about some of her paranormal experiences. Sophia McDonald was born in the mountain country of middle Tennessee in the early years of the 20th century. Around the age of four or five, her father passed away while serving in the infantry in World War I. Shortly thereafter the family moved to northwestern Kentucky in the "land between the rivers" (now known as the "land between the lakes"). Sometimes referred to as mountainous, in reality it was hill country; the mountains weren't very tall, as mountains go.

On a bright sunny spring day, Sophia, a very young girl of about five or six but full of vim and vinegar as little girls often are, went into the mountains with Claude, an older relative who was around 17 or 18. He had completed high school, or more likely had dropped out; at least, he was not in school on this day. They had gone to the mountains for a picnic, just for the fun of it. Readying lunch in a clearing in a heavy timbered area, Claude had laid back to relax as Sophia began to run about as young girls have a wont to do, chasing seen and unseen butterflies, bees, and the like.

Claude called asking her to stop and sit down and eat. As they were eating, he began to tell her that the area where they were had long been an Indian burial ground—at least that was the local legend, and most folks believed it to be true. The time when burials had taken place was in the far distant past, but the area was still considered to be sacred.

Suddenly both of them were startled; Sophia dropped her fried chicken and Claude spilled his iced tea as a group of fairies appeared from nowhere and danced across the clearing, disappearing just as quickly as they had appeared. Sophia knew they were fairies because they looked like the pictures in the storybooks her mother sometimes read to her at bedtime.

Before Sophia and Claude could regain their composure, an Indian appeared out of nowhere, just as the fairies had. He was dressed in full gear, including a feathered headdress. Without speaking a word, the Indian reached down into the earth and brought out some roots, gesturing for Claude and Sophia to try some. Sophia refused with violent head shaking. It was a different story with Claude; it seems he would try anything. With one bite, he began to act weird, dancing around and acting silly. He had never acted that way before.

Claude's actions scared Sophia so badly that she began to run. She never considered that she did not know the way home and they were a long way away— she just ran. Even after she arrived home, she was not sure how she got there. However, in typical fashion, her mother met her at the kitchen door with a scolding, announcing Sophia was late—too late for supper, in fact. She was sent straight to bed. Sophia tried to explain what had happened, to no avail.

Claude was never seen again after the incident—or if he was, no one would talk about it.

Several years later, when Sophia was about 16, she found herself in the same place where the events with Claude had taken place. During all those years, she had told no one about her experience. She had not forgotten about it, but she had never repeated it to a single soul. Occasionally, someone would ask about Claude, but that was all.

This time, she was with Seth, a casual boyfriend; they had been out for an afternoon car ride and ended there. For reasons unknown to her, she began to tell him about the strange event that had occurred so long ago. The same trees were there, along with the same bushes.

Seth was something of a practical joker. He didn't believe the story, but he started to dance around acting silly, thinking it would be fun to scare Sophia. She was at peace with the world resting and looking up through the tree limbs as the sun played hide-and-seek among them. Her request to "Please stop!" was met with more dancing and shouts, kind of like the calls Seth believed real Indians made when on the warpath. The more Sophia pleaded, the wilder Seth danced and the sillier he acted.

More begging made no difference; it just made him act sillier. As a part of the demonstration, he raised a large stone. Immediately, a large furry animal rushed out and ran headlong across the clearing, and over Sophia's leg, disappearing before reaching the trees on the other side. Neither could determine what it was. They knew it was not a bear, although there was an occasional bear in the area. Other animals were ruled out as well—squirrels, rabbits, dogs, or any other creatures either had ever seen.

Both of them freaked out. Sophia flailed about screaming, "Get me out of here!" Seth had stopped trying to be funny, wishing he had not come into the area. He was ready to leave.

Nighttime comes quickly in the mountains. It seemed as if a switch had turned off the sun. Apparently several hours had passed, but neither realized the passing of time. They knew the mountain was no place to be in the dark, especially with no light from the moon or stars. Somehow they found the car and then found the trail to the road with which they had entered.

For a few minutes, a feeling of comfort settled in, that is until they rounded the first bend. Up ahead, a fog or cloud of some kind floated a few feet above the road. It just stayed there with no fog anywhere else. Seth braked to a stop wondering how to pass. Something told him that whatever it was, it was not natural. Sophia would have none of that as she frantically beat Seth's shoulder with demands to "Get me off this mountain, get me off right now!" Seth also wanted to go, but fear wouldn't permit it.

Slowly the car inched forward, but the fog didn't move from the middle of the roadway. Slowly Seth moved to the left to bypass it. It also moved left. He tried moving right, but the fog followed.

Then a long, thin projection sprouted from the fog. It seemed to be beckoning with a "come closer" motion. That was the last thing either Sophia or Seth wanted to do.

"Go past that thing! Do it now!"

"I'm not sure what that thing is. I can't get past!"

"Yes you can! Do it right now, I don't care, get me out of here!"

Features seemed to appear as they drove closer. "Something's not right with that thing, it's spooky." By this time hysteria was rampant.

"That thing's trying to tell us something!" screamed Sophia. "Hit the gas and get us out of here!"

The car leaped forward toward the thing, which parted as they drove through, and the features became clear. "That's Claude in there, I'd know him any-where!"

There was no conversation the rest of the way home; both were too scared to talk, barely able to think. Reaching home, Sophia's mother was waiting as usual. This time was different; Sophia was pale and shaky, and it was obvious that something was wrong.

"What's the matter?"

It was several minutes before anything came out, at which time, the entire story was told. This time was different. All Mom said was, "I know; I've seen that thing. We've all seen it, but we don't discuss it."

—*Phillip Wells,*
Dellwood, Mo.

Animal spirits

At one time or another, we have all heard or maybe even shared the belief that animals can see ghosts and otherworldly entities in frequencies that we as humans cannot. Most people have seen their pets bark or hiss madly at seemingly nothing, sit and stare into space as though captivated by an invisible entity, or lick the air in the void as though reaching out to a disembodied hand.

Within this territory often follow questions pertaining to the afterlife of our furry friends. Do they go where we go or someplace else? If they can see the spirits of others, do they have souls like ours and would all the same rules apply? Do they seek out their loved ones or haunt certain locations and can they have unfinished business, keeping them earthbound after death?

While the questions are many, the answers often boil down to one, simple, yes. Give it a rest. Really, we humans are nothing but glorified animals ourselves, and to discount the value of our beloved pets would be a dire mistake. Animals, like humans, have dreams and feelings, a heart and a soul and can love as intensely as any other. Anthropocentric universal existence as one larger drama is the key to all life and matter in the universe. In the base mind and the Source exist the eternal seed—the building blocks of life—and within this core, value is intrinsic and inclusive. Here are some of the stories relating to the intrinsic existence of the soul, regardless of what earthly vessel that soul may have once existed within.

Big White Dog

When I was a young girl, I was a member of a group called "Brownies." The troop building was not far from my school. This incident took place during the winter. It was so very cold and raining. It seemed the wind was always blowing. On this particular day I had walked home after school, and, as I was doing my homework, I remembered my Brownie meeting. I rushed to my bedroom and put on my uniform. By now it was pouring down rain. I put the hood of my coat over my head and walked out the front door. I then ran as fast as I could to the troop building.

I was soaked by the time I arrived on the front porch. Nobody was there. I checked the front door and it was locked. It was either the wrong day or I was late for the meeting. The place was deserted.

I decided to sit on the front porch for a little while in hopes that the rain would let up. As I sat there, I noticed that a big car kept circling the block. I knew the man who drove the car and what business he was in. He was not a friend of my father's.

He drove around the park a few times, then parked by the side of the building. He walked over to where I was sitting, and told me that my father asked him to pick me up and drive me home. I knew that was not true, so I thanked him and told him I'd rather walk home.

By this time it was pitch dark, and I was scared because of that man. The rain had let up, so I started to walk home.

In the park near the road, there were three head-stones all with the same family name. I stopped briefly to look at them. When I turned around, there was the man parked with the passenger door open. Now I was scared. I didn't trust him. I told him again that I'd rather walk, but he grabbed my arm.

At that moment, a huge, beautiful white dog—it looked like a German Shepherd—came from my left side. The dog kept his back legs on the ground, and got right in the man's face, baring its teeth. Immediately the man let go. I lost my footing and fell backward. When I looked up, the man was speeding away in his car, the passenger door still open.

The dog was licking me all over my face. I couldn't stop hugging this beautiful creature. He made me feel so safe. He had the most beautiful eyes. It was as though he could see through my soul. The beautiful white dog walked me home. I kept my hand resting on the back of his neck, feeling so safe.

A neighbor friend of ours was getting out of his pickup, and he said "hi" to me. We arrived at my house and I opened the garage door. The white dog stayed with me. I told him to stay, as I went into the house to get him a blanket and something to eat. I turned around and hugged and kissed him again.

I hurried into the house, gathering the items together. When I walked out into the garage, the dog was not there. I looked, but he was nowhere to be found. I saw my footprints on the cement, but there were no paw prints. I could see our friend was still outside, grabbing items out of the back of his pickup. I walked over and asked if he had seen the big white dog that was with me. "No honey, I didn't see any dog with you," he said.

—*Dolly Smith*
Location withheld

Phantom Cat

One night in January 2003 as I sat in my living room watching TV, I thought I heard a noise in the kitchen—as if a cat had jumped on one of the stools at the counter. The kitchen and living room were divided by a wall with an open, arched doorway leading from one room to the other. It was easy to hear any noises from the kitchen while in the living room.

I was alone in the house, except for my roommate (who had retired for the night to his bedroom at the back of the house) and our three cats. We had no pet doors in the house, and none of the windows were open. One of my cats, a brown sealpoint, was outside; my white Persian was asleep in the living room where I could see her; and the third cat, a black mix who we called Jett, was kept in a spare bedroom because my Persian liked to beat her up. There wasn't any way for Jett to get out of the bedroom unless someone opened the door for her.

I got up to investigate the strange noise. Standing at the doorway looking into the kitchen, I saw what I thought was Jett sitting on one of the stools. On second glance I realized it was a bigger, blacker cat. I had not turned on the light yet, but the cat seemed to stand out in the darkness; it was somehow "blacker than black."

The black cat jumped onto the kitchen counter and casually walked over to the sink. It walked onto the windowsill over the sink and sat down with its back to me looking out the window. Then it seemed to become aware of my presence, and turned its head to look at me. I remember thinking what a pretty face it had, but in the next second its face became the most malevolent, evil-looking face I'd ever seen. I had the horrible feeling that it wanted to fly across the room and rip out my throat.

Shaken, I immediately switched on the kitchen light and no cat was visible. I moved closer to the sink to look, but nothing was there. I then checked on Jett and found her sound asleep in the bedroom.

I immediately told my roommate about the strange cat, but he had no explanation for it either.

Last year, right before my Nana (Vera Casey) passed away, she told me that one night a big black cat had jumped up onto her bed, walked onto her chest, and sat there looking at her. The cat vanished before her eyes. I told her about my own phantom cat experience. She told me the cat's coloring seemed to stand out in the darkness of the room—the same thing I had thought when I saw the cat in my kitchen. My Nana lived in an assisted senior condo community where pets were forbidden, so no one had any cats there.

I've often wondered if there was a purpose or reason for this cat's appearance in my house or my Nana's house.

—*Judy Stemen,*
Bloomington, Calif.

Comforting Mommy

February 2005 was a bad month for the Steed family. My brother-in-law Randy passed away on February 15, and I awoke two days later to discover that our guinea pig Wallace had died in his sleep. I immediately went into shock because there was no warning. Even though Wallace was going to turn six in April, he was active and played right up to his death. My husband Richard even heard him up eating during the night.

Wallace looked so natural, lying there like he was sleeping. I picked him up and held him, crying, "Why didn't you tell Mommy you were going away?"

Boots, our hamster, went nuts scratching on his aquarium's glass, wanting to be picked up as well. He loved Wallace so much that he'd imitate him like any human little brother would do in admiration of his elder.

We buried Wallace in the backyard in a wooden box, wrapped in a blanket with some of his favorite toys. I let Boots look upon him before we did. That Saturday I brought home some flowers from Randy's funeral and placed them on Wallace's grave. I also kept a vigil to make sure that the neighborhood cats didn't dig him up.

For a number of days after Wallace's death, I felt this softness near my left arm. Whenever I held Wallace, he always cradled his head on that elbow or climbed up onto my shoulder. I was sitting at the computer about a week later and I felt his nose touch my knee. One of the ways he gave kisses was to put his muzzle up to my lips and touch me for a few minutes. If he happened to be cranked with energy at the time, I'd feel this penetrating surge. I felt that when he touched my knee.

Then on March 6, I glanced over at his large aquarium and he was standing there looking at me. I was lying on the couch because I was sick with a virus at the time. He had that same loving, concerned look he always got when I was sick and he wanted to comfort me.

It was weird because the sighting barely registered with me at the time since I still expected him to be there. When the realization set in that he was dead, not more than a few minutes later, I looked back and he had vanished. I haven't seen or felt him since. I think he just wanted to assure himself that I was going to be okay with his passing and with the illness I was suffering. I think he also wanted me to know that it was okay that we'd gotten another guinea pig (Pippin) to keep me company at night when my husband worked.

Pippin was lying there in bed when Wallace appeared and never showed the slightest reaction. The most bizarre part of this whole incident is that Pippin displays the behaviors of both Rheagan (the guinea pig we had before Wallace) and Wallace, and has seemed to learn quicker than either of them. My husband and

I have often wondered if his older brothers have been coaching him while we sleep!

—Kelly Steed,
Marion, Ohio

Sky

Animals have always been a very special part of my life, and a number of years ago, I'd even tried breeding Siamese cats. But that was then and this is now, and lately I've found myself looking forward to a relatively pet-free existence when my beloved dogs eventually depart this earth. Somehow, though, I could never imagine life without a cat. I was hoping my shy, black house cat, "Puddy," would provide companionship for me as I enjoyed the rewards of maturity. Then I had a dream which changed all that.

In the dream, my dearly beloved, long-deceased Siamese mother cat, "Ribbons," appeared to me. Ribbons had left us for the spirit world about 15 years previously after a long life during which she bore many litters of beautiful kittens, most of them purebred Siamese like herself. But purebred or not, we either placed them in good, loving homes or kept them ourselves. I was also a young mother at the time, and Ribbons and I seemed to understand one another instinctively. We were quite close for her entire, mercifully long life, during which we shared two cross-country moves and many unforgettable adventures. Only a person who has had a truly special relationship with a beloved pet can understand what we shared. When she died, I buried her in the backyard and cried for three days.

In my dream, she appeared as a mother cat with nursing kittens. (Again!) I noted that her hair was a little longer than it had been during her lifetime with me (Siamese cats have short hair), but she had the same seal-point markings. I also noticed that she looked thin and unhealthy. She told me she was dying and asked if she could come back to live with me. I replied sadly that I now had two dogs and another cat who needed my attention, and felt that her strong personality wouldn't fit the dynamics of our home at this time. I asked if she could look around for another place to live.

She didn't reply, but simply vanished as the dream faded to black and ended. I mentioned my dream to several friends because I've only rarely received communication from the animal or pet spheres, even though I've been a practicing Spiritualist medium and professional psychic for many years.

It was perhaps a month later that I heard from Ribbons again. This time there was no visual image, only her voice in a dream that said, "I'm coming." Something strong and instinctive inside of me responded instantly, and I replied from the depths of my being, "Honey, come on!" I sensed that she had nowhere else to go and that she needed me desperately now. I was also reminded of how strong-minded she'd been, and I knew she wouldn't hesitate to make demands of me when necessary. I'd always been there for her when she really needed me, and nothing would ever change that.

After Ribbons' last message, I began to look around, wondering when and where I might find her. I attended a local cat show, and searched the classified ads, animal shelters, and pet stores. I chased down every lead, but no cat or kitten seemed to belong to me. Then I remembered Ribbons' exact words. She'd said, "I'm coming!" not "Come and get me." So I decided to stop looking and wait to see what, if anything, would happen. It didn't take long—about 15 weeks (the gestation and minimum nursing time for kittens).

Then one afternoon, two ladies who were close friends came to my home for readings. As they were about to leave, one of them hesitated and turned to me before stepping over the threshold. It seemed as if an invisible hand had tapped her on the shoulder. "Oh!" she said. "Do you need a kitten?"

I admitted I'd been looking, but made no promises because I wasn't seeking just any cat; it had to be my cat, and no other! They explained that one of them had a calico mother cat with a litter in which no two kittens were alike. They decided that one particular kitten, a long-haired calico, seemed especially right for me. I broke my resolve and offered to drive out to see the litter, hoping to have a better selection, but the owner said that her home in the country was difficult to find and insisted it would be easier and more convenient for her to bring the kitten to me when she made her next visit to town.

True to her word, two weeks later I received a call saying she would be driving in and could bring the calico kitten with her if I were still interested. I asked if she could bring several of them for me to select from, and my heart sank when she replied, "Well, I guess I could bring the other one."

I had little hope that a kitten with Siamese markings would be among such a litter because Siamese genes are recessive. In the all-too-many accidental litters Ribbons had produced with friendly but definitely un-Siamese neighborhood cats, to my great disappointment, not one kitten ever carried her regal markings.

But when they arrived, and I looked into the little carrier placed squarely in the center of my living room, I saw that the "other" kitten was a beautiful, perfectly formed seal-point Siamese, with hair just slightly longer than that of a purebred. The omens were too strong for me to deny. I hadn't even had to step outside of my front door to find her; she had come home to me just as she'd said she would! I picked up my little kitten and held her in my hands. As I looked again for the first time into her beautiful blue eyes, I renamed her "Sky," for the heavenly pathway she had used to find her way home.

Six months after Sky returned home, she had made fast friends with both of my dogs and my other cat Puddy, despite their (and my own) original mis-givings. And now, four years later, our dogs have left us for the spirit world and Puddy spends her long, lei-surely days on the chaise lounge while Sky follows me around from room to room and into the garden as I work, watching from her high perch, pacing back and forth when she's restless, stretching out on top of my paperwork when she needs attention, punishing me with rejection, rewarding me with mice, and generally letting me know her wants and needs. We're a pair, we two. It's good to have her home again.

—*Saphira Dil Rain,*
Kansas City, Mo.

A Smart Dog

In the early 1950s my father inherited a farm from his deceased parents. The farm was located in Johnson County, Indiana, about 35 miles from Indianapolis. Every Sunday he would drive down to the farm just to check up on it. He had a smooth-haired little mixed breed dog that traveled with him on the front seat of his '39 Plymouth.

Each time he visited the farm he would pass the cemetery where his parents were buried and the little dog would hear him say "Hi Mom, Hi Dad," as he passed the cemetery. The dog could barely see out of the high car windows.

We all know that our pets cannot read newspapers or do algebra, but they seem very aware of other things. On one trip as he passed the cemetery, he did not say "Hi Mom, Hi Dad," and the little dog stood up, looked at him, and barked!

—*Arthur E. Thompson,*
Pompano Beach, Fla.

The Cat Came Back

By 1991, the last of my sister Maggie's children had gotten married and begun families of their own. Both she and her husband, Al, were planning to retire within the next few years. I suppose that their house seemed terribly empty. So Maggie and Al adopted two new kittens. One was black and white spotted and was named Patches. According to my sister, the other was exactly the color of sherry. Thus, she acquired that name. Both cats had been spayed or neutered and began very pampered lives.

In October 1995, Al and Maggie sold their house in California and purchased a new one in Hayden, Idaho. Both had retired and were ready for a change. They were delighted with their new home. So were the cats. This house had a fireplace, which was a novelty, and quite a contrast to California. The cats were especially fond of lying on the hearth and soaking up the warmth.

All during 2001, Sherry appeared to be ailing and wasting away. There were numerous trips to the vet, vitamins, and so on. But on December 5, she passed on.

Al and Maggie were concerned that Patches might grieve himself to death over the loss of his sister. However, that never happened. After his family had gone to bed, Patches could be heard pouncing about in the den. His owners assumed that he was playing with his favorite toy, a fake mouse.

During the latter part of May 2002, Al noticed a white spot at the back of the fireplace. He thought that was strange because they had not built any fires recently. By June 1, a perfect image of Sherry was displayed there. I visited my sister during the last week of September and took pictures. This image was complete with eyes, whiskers, and everything.

We assumed that the image would disappear whenever fires were being built again. Strangely enough, that never happened. The image remained throughout the winter and on to the present.

At age 12, Patches is a senior citizen and pretty neurotic. But he can still be heard pouncing in the den after his family has retired for the night.

—Mary Crawford,
Dutton, Ala.

Christmas Ghost Wolf

It was the Saturday before Christmas in 2003. My wife and I had just left the home of some relatives living in rural Elbert County, Georgia, driving north on Highway 17. We settled in for the two-hour drive home. The cold, foggy darkness fell across the mildly hilly landscape. To our right was scrub brush just on our side of an old railroad track. To the left was forest broken by the occasional home site.

It was after 9:00 p.m., and traffic was sparse. There was a car about 200 feet in front of us. As paranormal investigators in our spare time, we usually kept at least one camera at the ready. But on this sleepy night, our cameras, along with Christmas presents, were in the trunk.

Just as we approached a darkened trailer park on the right beyond the railroad tracks we both felt compelled to look at the left side of the road. We saw something rush out in front of us from the left. A car, one of the few out that evening, passed us going the other way and immediately slowed down, then kept moving.

We first thought it was a dog we were about to hit. Then it dawned on us the "dog" had shoulders higher than the hood of our car. It had a large wolfen head, fangs, flowing hair, and a huge body. We were aghast when we realized we could see through it. The taillights of the car in front of us were clearly visible through the massive beast.

The shaggy, long-tailed "dog" turned and glanced at us, then faded out of view as it reached the right side of the road. And it was gone—not gone as if it had run off; it simply faded away. This all happened in a matter of seconds.

Just up ahead on the left was a well-lit rural post office for the small community of Dewey Rose. We parked under the lone light there and stopped. We were both shaken up, excited, and curious. If that had been an animal it was impossible for us not to have struck it. And any four-legged animal like that would not be that large or swift—or opaque.

After getting our wits about us we returned to the site where we had seen the crossing happen. After removing our cameras from the trunk, we examined the ground closely with flashlights. There was no evidence of any prints on the ground. The pets at the trailer park were quiet. Anything as large as what we had seen would surely have started up a ruckus. A coating of dew from the fog clung to the bushes along both sides of the roadway. We saw no evidence that any of it had been disturbed.

So what did we see—a ghost, a really large animal, a werewolf, Indian spirit, or what else? The car in the oncoming lane had seen it too, or it would not have slowed down, so we knew we had seen something.

This occurred in the vicinity of the Georgia Guidestones, an area the Indians have called "the center of the world," as well as numerous earthlights we had seen and investigated ourselves. Rumors abound of pagan, Celtic, and other groups practicing in the area. Could our mystery beast have been something conjured up by one of these groups? We may never know.

—*Steve Golden,*
Duluth, Ga.

Spirit Guides and Angels

When I was a boy, still certain of my invincibility and endlessly inquisitive, while off somewhere in the New Mexican desert, I climbed a cliff side, alone and without protective gear or harnesses. As one might expect, at some point I found myself stuck, without any grips or fissures to work with, some 20 feet above a ragged assortment of rocks and debris. I was petrified—and miles away from anyone who could help. Then I made the mistake of trying to turn around, placing my heels on the small footholds I had and trembling from head to toe.

Looking down for my next course of action, I suddenly found myself in a blur, tumbling and falling. To my amazement, when I opened my eyes, I was sitting somehow between two jutting spikes of stone, seemingly unscathed. To this day, I have no explanation for what saw me safely to the ground.

Was it lady luck or something else? Could Guardian Angels really exist? The flurry of questions I faced was only outpaced by my sheer amazement and gratitude to be alive.

While I, myself, never grasped a definitive answer, thousands of letters have reached FATE over the decades attesting to the definite existence of an Angelic race, putting down roots somewhere in the universe and coming to help the mortal in their most troubling of moments. Here are just a few of those gems, giving testament to assurance that we aren't alone and are indeed, loved.

We Are Never Alone at Death

In 1982, my husband suddenly walked out on my two sons and me. I was 36 and quite desperate as to what to do. My training was in the art field, but I could find no jobs in my area. I had been out of the work force for 14 years as a wife and mother.

I learned of a part-time job taking care of an elderly woman named Vi in her home three days a week from 7:00 a.m. to 5:00 p.m. I applied and got the position.

Each day after my shift with Vi was over, a registered nurse came in who fed her, got her ready for bed,
and slept with her through the night. When I arrived,
breakfast would be in progress. Other days and nights,
two other caregivers alternated being with her.

Vi sat in her wheelchair each day. She barely
spoke, but I did whatever I could to entertain her and
tend to her needs. I read to her, wheeled her about,
served lunch, and directed her attention to the deer
in the fields, the birds in the trees, and other outside
nature activities.

After seven months I saw her condition deterio-
rating. The nurse would give me daily briefs as to care
guidelines when I came in. She informed me each
morning that she didn't think Vi would live through
the coming day. I would arrive hoping she would have
passed easily in her sleep, but each day upon arriving,
there was Vi eating her morning oatmeal. She kept
clinging to life, much to the surprise of everyone.

"Amazing," said the nurse. "All indications are she
should have gone days ago."

At any rate, the nurse gave me instructions about
getting in touch with her if Vi died and calling the
ambulance team. Inwardly, I prayed that Vi would
hang on just one more day. I had never even been to
a funeral at that point in my life, and I had never seen
a dead person. Fear crept in; I worried that I would be
helpless or faint if she died while I was there.

I sat down by Vi and began serving her oatmeal. It was no more than five minutes after the nurse left that she pushed the spoon away. I tried again to feed her. She pushed my hand away again. She took both hands and held the tray of her wheelchair. Her head bowed down. I heard a distinct rattle.

Oh my God, I cried within. That's the death rattle! I was a prolific reader, and this phrase was often mentioned in stories and novels I had read.

Instinctively, I rose and went behind Vi's chair. I gently pulled her back so I could cradle her head and body against my chest and embrace her. I was shaking inside and praying for her. It was the only thing I could do. Within a few minutes her body shuddered and went limp.

As I continued to hold Vi, a beautiful light began to appear around us. To my amazement, I saw three figures appear in the mist-like light, two females and a male. I saw both of Vi's arms reach up to them in spirit. They reached their arms to her.

The vision soon faded. I was deeply affected by what I had seen. Still in a daze, I gently left Vi slumped over on the wheelchair tray and called the nurse and the ambulance. In minutes they arrived. They all were so efficient, working as a team at a ritual repeated hundreds of times as they removed her body to the hospital or funeral home. As they wheeled her out the door I sat down and bawled. I felt so many things at once: relief; the shock of being so close to a death for the first time; the looming question of how to feed my kids now that my job was done; and the sadness of losing my quiet, cute little friend of seven months.

A young male attendant about 28 years old came over. He put his hand on my shoulder ever so gently. "This is your first, isn't it?" he asked.

"Yes!" I sobbed.

"I know. I did the same when it first occurred for me." A warm squeeze on my shoulder, and my comforter was gone.

Is it true then that there is a life after? Many have written of seeing loved ones at death reaching out or calling to deceased relatives. I had several paranormal experiences and dreams prior to this, but never anything like that.

Though I had dreaded and shuddered at the thought Vi would die on my watch, I was enriched deeply by this experience, not only because I believe Vi wanted me to be the one to die with, but to have seen several deceased relatives reach out to her at death confirmed what I had read for years, that you are never alone when you die.

—*Joyce Benedict,*
Hyde Park, N.Y.

Angel on the Wall

Every fall my mother, Gail Cross, spends a few weeks with our family in Texas. The year 2001 was no different. We all had a nice time and took many pictures at Thanksgiving.

When my mother returned home, my brother Max picked her up and they stopped by his house. Mom had only one picture left on a roll of film in her camera. She wanted to finish the roll so it could be developed. Mom had told us about a flag Max had painted on his house, so she took a picture of it.

When the pictures were developed, she sent me a copy of them. A few days ago I was putting some pictures in an album. As I do this, I always inspect each picture because it is not unusual for me to have strange things appear in pictures I take. When I was looking at the picture of Max's house, I noticed something above the flag. When my mom called that weekend, I asked her if the wall above the flag is solid white, or does it have a faded spot? She assured me it is all white. I told her she got a picture of a ghost right above the flag.

She got her picture out, and she saw it too. The next day she showed the picture to my brother and told him about the ghost above the flag. Max looked at it and said, "That's an angel, not a ghost."

Mom took the picture to the senior center where she eats lunch and showed it to her friends. They all felt it was an angel.

I took the photo album out to look at the picture again. My husband was looking at it, and he agreed, "They're right. It's an angel. There is the head and it has its right wing raised. The left wing is down at its side."

I wonder who this angel is. Is it Max's guardian angel, or my sister-in-law Janet's? Or perhaps it is Mom's Guardian Angel, waving to her as if to say, "I got you safely home again."

—*Polly Hammarlund,*
Harker Heights, Tex.

Auspicious Developments

Throughout my entire life I have had the feeling that one of God's angels was looking over me.

I am now 65. In 1953, when I was about ten, I moved with my mother—Virginia Halzda, a single mom—from Pennsylvania to New York. My aunts were nurses at a hospital on the corner from our brownstone apartments in Brooklyn. My mother got a job at the same hospital, working in the office all night.

Although my cousins were in the apartment above, and our wonderful landlord who looked out for us was downstairs, I was alone in our one-and-a-half-room apartment at night.

I was afraid of the dark and of going blind, and if I couldn't see some kind of light through the window at night, I would panic.

One very dark night, I was having a panic attack when the face of a beautiful woman, surrounded by light, smiled down on me. I became calm immediately. I saw the door to the apartment open and close, and went off to sleep. I have never been afraid of the dark since.

In 1967, I had a strong impulse to write to my favorite uncle, Merle Fine. I hadn't heard from or seen him for years. He passed away a week after receiving my letter.

In June 1986, my son Mark and I were traveling from Florida. I was pulling a trailer and my son was following in his car. I had gotten on the wrong high-way, and had to turn around. We took an exit and had pulled into a dirt drive behind a mall, when I lost my steering. If I had stayed on the highway, I would have been in a severe accident, possibly involving my son and other people on the highway. If that isn't proof someone is up there watching over me, there never will be any.

So many other unusual occurrences, too numerous to write about here, have happened since then that I know that my angel is still there, looking out for me.

—*Mrs. M. Vicidomini,*
Harrington Del.

Strange but Friendly Encounters

I believe in angels. I have heard one, and I have touched one.

I had for some time believed there must be angels because so many times in traffic and at home I was saved from accidents. One afternoon I was taking a nap, and I was very deeply asleep when, from a great distance, I heard a soft voice with an accent calling my name, over and over. I remember emerging from a deep place within. That voice calling my name became louder until I awoke. I felt very sure that the soft voice had called me back.

My next encounter with my angel, whom I thought of as "Alice," occurred one afternoon when I was resting on my bed. I heard several people open the screen door of my lanai and cross into the living room. After opening the door, the voices sounded like a group of young people laughing and talking gaily to one another.

"Who can it be?" I thought. "I just don't know any people that happy."

I jumped off the bed and crossed the hall to see them leaving through the door of the large sitting room. I saw them dressed in rather short, brightly colored dresses and pants. As they disappeared into the room, one girl called over her shoulder, "Stay close to home, Lois." A few seconds later, I reached the long living room and it was empty. They had vanished.

The next strange encounter happened this past winter. We had one cold weekend, and I located a fur jacket worn long ago and put it on to wear to a concert. Rita, a neighbor, picked me up. I went in to the concert hall first while she parked the car. I always sit in the second row from the front as I want to see the instruments played and hear everything. When I reached my row of seats, there in the aisle seat sat a very old lady with a fur jacket like mine. I brushed around her and sat down. After a minute or two she grabbed my hand. What a grip! It felt as though a prizefighter had a grip on me, but it didn't hurt. She really held on.

I looked down at the hand holding mine, and I was startled to see it was white and pink, the color of a baby's. I gently tried to ease my hand out of her grip, but she held on. Finally, she released her tight grip.

My neighbor arrived. I moved over and my friend was between me and the old lady. I watched her for some time. The music began. I looked back at the old lady, but her seat was empty. No one was there. No one had gone up the aisle. I waited for intermission to question my friend. She said, "She was there, and then she wasn't there. She was gone!"

At the time of the memorial for my husband, another strange thing happened. Family and a few friends had gathered at our cabin in Clyde, North Carolina. My husband loved Queen Anne's lace. It had grown very sparsely in our neighborhood. We had none on our property. Suddenly, the morning of our simple ceremony, we had Queen Anne's lace from the beginning of our long curving driveway all the way to the steps of the house—a mass of wildflowers.

So many other things happen that are difficult to understand, but I have seen, felt, and on several other occasions also have experienced an angel's presence. For me, they are very real and constantly near us. I think the old lady whose hand felt like a prizefighter must have been around when I had some very near-misses while driving.

—Lois Allen,
Englewood, Fla.

Guardian Angels

As a little girl I always asked God in my night prayers to send Guardian Angels to care for me. In my later years I still asked for protection with the angels. Somehow it seemed to give me the strength I needed in so many things. In all my 91 years I still said this prayer and believed.

On December 1, 2003, I felt a twinge and fluttering in my heart. Feeling rather weak and unsteady, I took to bed. For a week I lay there, feeling these were to be my last days on earth. I didn't even bother to eat. As I lay in bed I prayed that God would take me quietly with no pain or discomfort—just let me sleep away.

My daughter stopped by and, seeing my condition, she telephoned my son. He and his wife took me to the hospital where I underwent many tests. I began to feel better and arrived home the day before Christmas. Again I prayed that God would send guardian angels to care for me.

The first night home I slept soundly. I awoke about three in the morning, and right next to my bed I saw two angels. Their wings were shining gold and their faces were beautiful. They wore long white gowns. One angel was taller than the other and stood behind the shorter one. Both angels had downcast eyes and their hands were folded in prayer. I felt so good knowing I had such protection and fell into a deep sleep.

Somehow when I awoke I felt much better. I had to return to the hospital for many more tests, but I went with faith and hope to remain here on earth. My tests proved okay and I returned home again with great faith in the supernatural.

God sent me those angels to let me know He was taking care of me. Oh yes, there are angels—if you have faith!

—*Lillian Burton,*
River Grove, Ill.

"Thanks, Dad!"

My father was a wonderful man and we were always very, very close. After he died suddenly at age 80, my mother went into the hospital for surgery. After that she was going into a nursing home so she asked me to sell the house for her. One day as I was decorating and cleaning it to put it on the market, I smelled a bad odor coming from the area near the front door. It smelled like rotting garbage.

There was a small throw rug where people wiped their feet when they came in. It looked clean, but I figured that it must have something bad on it, so I threw it out. The smell continued. Later, I thought it must be coming from the hall carpet. It looked clean, but I shampooed it anyway. The smell continued for days.

There was a heating grill close by and I thought maybe some food had fallen down there, or perhaps there was a dead mouse in it.

I took the grill off and looked all around with a flashlight and a mirror. The duct was perfectly clean. By the way, while this was going on, my wife could smell nothing, but to me it was very strong.

The smell continued for days. Next, I thought the smell must be coming right through the floor from the basement.

The house foundation was poorly built, with gaping holes where the floor joists sat in notches cut into the blocks. It was so bad that one time a squirrel got into the basement. I went downstairs to look for a dead animal.

On the underside of the joists, my dad had nailed a small board to make a shelf. Getting on a stool and using a flashlight, I looked over the shelf to the wall where there was a hole in the block. I saw something. I pulled it out. It was a wallet with a big wad of bills.

This was very typical of my father, as he was a bit of a worrywart and was always prepared for any emergency. When I found the money, the smell stopped immediately.

With the money I bought a large framed print that I couldn't afford before. It hangs over my fireplace.

When I look at it and enjoy it, I say, "Thanks, Dad!"

—*Bruce Collings,*
Hamilton, Ontario, Canada

Liz's Friends

In 1955, when my daughter Liz arrived, she did not come alone.

She spent her first few months in a bassinet beside our bed, and several unseen entities spent their time standing around the bassinet. Because I was getting up at night to tend to her, I left a nightlight burning. There always seemed to be a presence around her— actually, it was more like a crowd.

It felt as though I had to shoulder my way through to get to her. Naturally, this wore on my nerves. It wasn't clear to me just who or what was sharing our space, but there was no doubt something was.

Finally, one night, I reached over to try to settle her down and saw that several smoke-like figures were clustered around the bassinet. This was too much for me. Rolling away toward my husband's side of the bed, I muttered, "Oh no, not again."

Bob was a very heavy sleeper, who under normal circumstances wouldn't wake up unless I shouted, and even then would take time to reach complete consciousness. This time, though, he quietly asked, "What's wrong?"

I didn't look at him, but buried my head in my pillow. "I can't stand it," I said. "There's always 'things' around her and I'm tired of it!"

"Don't you know who they are?" he asked softly. "They are spirits who came with her to watch over her; they are friends."

"I don't care," I replied. "I don't want to deal with them, I want them to go away."

He didn't answer, and I got up to see to the baby, telling the visitors silently, "Go away—you make me nervous!"

They didn't go, but from that time they were more circumspect around me, and that was good enough. As Liz grew older and moved into her own room, they spent their time there. I would go in to get her up from a nap, and find her watching things I couldn't see. Later she would "talk" with them in her baby babble. I couldn't see anyone, but she certainly did. I still had the sense that she wasn't alone.

One afternoon when she was two, I found her standing in her crib chatting away with "someone." She turned to me, pointing to the empty space next to her.

"Kitties, mama, kitties!"

Apparently, her guests had brought kittens for her to play with.

As Liz grew older, the crowd seemed to thin, and at age four they seemed to be gone, or she had learned to be discreet about them. Who or what they were, I can only guess.

Now a grown woman with a daughter of her own, who quite often says startling things, Liz is still very psychic. Is she an "old soul," who brought friends with her? I can't say positively, but I believe she is.

I can say that her father denied absolutely that he had ever said anything to me about spirits—asleep or awake—and refused to believe any part of it.

So who explained the situation to me in that soft, calming voice?

—*Sylvia W. Hutchins,*
Bellingham, Wash.

Mrs. Miller's Christmas Story

One year, as Christmas approached, I was decorating a small tree in the den of my house. I was a schoolteacher, and Christmas break was a time to regroup and prepare to finish the school year. There came a knock on my door. It was the school bus driver, Mrs. Miller, whom I had known most of my life. She had driven the school bus I rode as an elementary student. That December day, she dropped by to deliver a batch of Christmas cookies. We sat down together and shared some cookies and coffee. Our conversation turned to memories of Christmas, and in particular, memories of children at Christmas. She told me this story:

There was a family who had lived on a farm in the community for years. They had three children. The youngest, a four-year-old boy, had been diagnosed with a kidney disease and did not have long to live. It was the Christmas season and the little boy had been admitted to the local hospital. His family was exhausted when Mrs. Miller stopped in to visit. She carried with her a copy of the children's story, The Littlest Angel. To give the family a much-needed break, she offered to stay with the little fellow for a while and read him the story. Grateful, the family stepped out for a bite to eat.

Mrs. Miller propped herself up in the hospital bed next to the child. He was especially glad to see her since she had a story to read him. Although extremely weak, he managed a smile. He followed the pictures diligently with his big brown eyes as she turned each page, reading aloud as only she could do in her tender but expressive voice.

When she had finished the story, she closed the book and asked him if he believed in angels. In a soft, thin voice, he affirmed that he did. She smiled and asked him how he knew this. He whispered to her, "because the littlest angel is right up there." He pointed in the direction of the ceiling directly above his bed. "And he wants me to go with him," he added.

Mrs. Miller stayed by his side as he rested, and soon the family returned. It was only a few minutes later that he opened his eyes, looked up, smiled, and then closed his eyes forever. In that moment, Mrs. Miller knew he was seeing the angel who had come to accompany him at the time of his passing.

I thanked Mrs. Miller for sharing such a special Christmas story with me.

As I waved goodbye to her at the door, something caught the corner of my eye. It was an old, yellowed Christmas card on the floor in front of the doorway. No doubt it had fallen out of a box of decorations I had maintained for years. I picked it up and looked inside to see who might have sent it. It bore no signature, had no note, and no envelope. Further, I had no memory of seeing it before. On the card was an ornate picture of a chubby little boy with wings and a halo. It was a little angel sent to me, I believe, by another little angel.

It has now been several years since Mrs. Miller too has passed. No doubt, a special angel came for her too. I have never doubted that the story she told me that afternoon was true.

—Donetta Briody,
Punta Gorda, Fla.

Mystery Woman or Guardian Angel?

In February 2000, I began providing day care for Mrs. Uda Hughes, who was 87 and living alone. She is a darling person, and I became very attached to her.

Usually, I would arrive at her home around 7:15 a.m. But on March 29, 2002, I had an uneasy feeling. I left early and arrived about 7:02. The door was locked, and I couldn't hear any sounds from inside. I had a key, so I unlocked the door and let myself in. I found Mrs. Hughes lying in the doorway of her bedroom. She was alert, but she couldn't get up. The strange thing was that she was not moaning or struggling. She seemed perfectly calm.

Since I weigh 110 pounds and she is considerably larger, I did not try to get her up. Instead, I phoned for help. Having completed my phone call, I came back and sat down beside her, thinking that I could comfort her until help arrived.

"Where did that woman go?" asked Mrs. Hughes.

I asked her whom she was talking about. She stated that she didn't know who she was, or how she got inside.

"What did she say to you?" I asked.

Mrs. Hughes told me that whoever the woman was, she was not anyone she knew. And that she never told her name nor even said a word. "She just pulled up a chair and sat down beside me!" Mrs. Hughes elaborated, "I could tell that she was a good person and that she wanted to help me."

Since I had unlocked the door myself, I knew that no one else had been there. So I suggested that perhaps it was Mrs. Hughes' Guardian Angel, who came to watch over her until I arrived. Mrs. Hughes just smiled and said, "You know, it might have been."

Some believe in guardian angels; others do not. I think this being was her guardian angel. Mrs. Hughes was far too calm and collected for any other explanation.

—Mary Crawford,
Dutton, Ala.

The Golden Staircase

I have never told anyone this story as I thought no one would believe me until now. What I saw 40 years ago was real, and still is to me today.

I was six years old. I got real sick that year with measles and chicken pox at the same time. Instead of putting me in the hospital, the doctor came to the house every day to check on me and give me shots, which I hated very much.

One night I developed a high fever. The doctor gave me a double dose of shots. He left with Mama, and I could hear them talking about me in the hall. The doctor told Mama he didn't think I would make it through the night. I became afraid, as I didn't know what was happening.

My room was dark except for the light coming in from the hallway. I looked across the room to the white wall above my dresser. An image appeared of a beautiful golden staircase. There were people in long white robes walking up and down the staircase. I realized they were angels. I watched them for a few minutes. I wondered where they were all going. They seemed to be in a hurry.

Then one of the angels stopped and looked at me. He smiled, and I smiled back at him. Then he went up the staircase and the image disappeared. I wasn't afraid anymore. I fell asleep, and sometime during the night my fever broke. I was so much better the next day that the doctor gave me medicine to take instead of giving me a shot. A few weeks later I was well again and back in school.

I never saw the golden staircase or the angels again. I am sure that the staircase is still out there somewhere, with the angels walking up and down going about their business.

—*Holly Simpson,*
Las Vegas, N. Mex.

The Healing Angel

I had just arrived at church on Easter Sunday, where I was scheduled to deliver the sermon. There were people behind me that I did not know. As I entered the church, one of the members called to me, "Charlie Brown, it's about time you got here." I was 15 minutes early, but they had expected me sooner.

A few minutes later, I was approached by a man who came up behind me. He asked if I was the same Charlie Brown that writes about angels. I told him I didn't know if I was the only one, but I did write about angels.

"Did you write one about 50 years ago about your brother?" he asked.

I paused in amazement. "Yes, I did," I replied. I had totally forgotten the story. It appeared in a magazine that I could no longer remember.

"I am Jimmy Ledbetter," the man told me. "I was with you when you shot your brother with the arrow. We were playing cowboys and Indians. You accidentally shot your brother in the eye." He paused in reflection.

As I walked up to the podium, I was taken back 50 years. It had been Easter Sunday when we were playing in the woods behind our home. I was 13. My two younger brothers and I were playing with Jimmy at our fortified cave about a mile behind our farm home. My brothers were soldiers defending the fort. Jimmy and I were attacking Indians with homemade bows and spears fashioned from local willow trees. We would shoot our arrows and when we ran out, we called a truce to retrieve them. No one expected anyone to get hurt. My last arrow struck my younger brother in the eye. Bobby started screaming and everyone panicked.

Religion was a daily practice in our household. I would even say my family was one of the worst examples of holy rollers that I had ever seen. My father drank and often came home drunk. My mother would continually pray that he would not come home in a crazed frenzy. We attended church every Sunday. We missed that Sunday because I was just getting over chicken pox: a reprieve for one Sunday out of 52.

I had always been impressed by the power of prayer. There was always someone who declared health problems or other maladies had been healed through prayer. I witnessed a crippled man throw down his crutches and walk, independent of any assistance.

"Gather around him" I shouted. "We have got to pray for him."

At 13, I wasn't too sure of how to pray. I was accustomed to church members jumping, shouting, and speaking in tongues. We placed our hands on Bobby and prayed the Lord's Prayer. I picked him up with the assistance of my other brother, Floyd. We started running up the hill to the highway. Old Doctor Coffey lived about half a mile away. We headed for his house.

Fortunately a neighbor stopped and drove us to his door. It was probably an hour before we got there. Mom and Dad were taking food to a sick friend and we could not reach them.

All the way, Bobby kept screaming that he could not see. I prayed all the way to the doctor and while he was being examined. I could hear the doctor trying to appease him. Nothing the doctor could say would help. The doctor cleaned the blood and came out to see me.

"Where did the blood come from?" he asked.

"It came from his eye where I shot him with an arrow," I replied.

The doctor scratched his head in total confusion. "There are signs of broken blood vessels in his eye, but no injury that would produce that amount of blood. Are you sure you hit him with an arrow?"

"Of course I did," I said. "I saw him pull the arrow out."

Finally Bobby settled down. The doctor kept telling him that there was no wound and that he was not blind.

We didn't have any money and the doctor said, "Well, I didn't have to sew him up, so I guess there is no charge." In those days, most of his house calls were paid for in kind. Few people had enough money for food. Doctor bills were unheard of. Unless we were bleeding to death, no one went to a doctor.

We began the trek back home. Bobby asked, "Who was the person who kept his hand on my eye while we were going to the doctor?"

I told him that no one held his eye. We were too busy simply getting him back to the main road.

"No," he replied. "Someone was beside me all the way to the doctor with his hand over my eye." He described a tall, glowing man dressed all in white.

"It must have been a healing angel," I told him. I felt cold chills run down my spine. This was a miracle and I was part of it.

I had heard of healing angels all my life. I had witnessed many healings in church. We even had roving preachers who would go house to house administering to the sick. Many of the bedridden would get out of bed, totally cured without the aid of a physician. I suppose that was why I was consumed by the urge to become an administrator for God.

This was 50 years ago to the day. The minister of the church, Margaret Ann Schmidt, had no idea that when she asked me to do the Easter Sunday sermon that it would be the culmination of a 50-year-old prayer.

As children, we think as children and act as children. When we are older, we put away childish things. Well maybe, just maybe, we shouldn't.

—*Charlie R. Brown*
Deland, Fla.

Eugene's Help

In 1994, my parents (Chuck and Sue Ostermeyer) and I were preparing to move from Los Angeles to Tucson, Arizona, since my dad's job was being transferred. There were many preparations to be made, one of which involved taking over a 14-foot boat Dad owned. I decided to accompany him on the drive over so Mom could continue packing up the household. This way we would be able to split up the driving.

So, on a date in mid-May, I took off a few days from my last college class at California State University–Northridge, with my professor's kind approval, and began to prepare for our road trip.

That night Dad came home exhausted from a business trip to Huntsville, Alabama. We began to prep the boat for our journey. Dad had carefully secured it in our driveway with a padlock. When we went to unlock it, we could not find the key. We scoured the house looking for any keys we could find. We tried each one, and none of them fit.

I could tell Dad was beginning to get a migraine from fatigue. He could not afford to be sick for this trip, so Mom and I urged him to go in and sleep. We would keep looking for the key.

Dad went off to the garage and came back with a hacksaw. He decided he would saw the lock off himself. After further urging, we convinced him to go in and rest. Mom and I continued to try other keys.

Later in the night, Mom emerged from the house with a cigar box that must have contained at least 100 different keys. I sat down next to the boat and began to try each one. After what seemed like an eternity, I was down to the last key. I reached in for it. My heart sank when I saw the word "GAS" stamped on it. It was a key for a gas cap, not a padlock. Nonetheless, I looked at it and at my watch. It was nearing midnight and I knew my dad would not have had enough sleep. I dreaded the idea of having to slowly cut through the padlock with a hacksaw, especially since we were all very tired and might easily have an accident. Despite the marking on the key, I tried it. It went into the lock, something none of the other keys had done, but did not budge.

I stared at the key and thought of my dear friend, Eugene Gintel. During college I had lucked out and gotten a part-time job at a family-owned pawnshop. At the time, it was wonderful because I had no car and was able to walk a only a few blocks to get to work. Eugene was the patriarch in the family. Having lost both of my beloved grandfathers six weeks apart at the age of three, Eugene became like a surrogate granddad to me. He was interested in everything, but especially good at fixing things. Items people would write off as broken forever found an extended life in his hands: toasters, fans, clocks, anything! There was nothing he couldn't fix. This was extremely helpful for his sons, Rudy and Ernest, who owned the pawnshop. He always had a tray of watches he was repairing. In a disposable age, he was endowed with a gift—giving an extended life to a product.

At this point, I was beginning to feel exhausted and a bit hopeless. I thought of Eugene. He'd passed away two years earlier and I still could picture him, upstairs in his little office overlooking the pawnshop. He'd be sitting at his desk with his tools spread neatly across the top, grinning from ear to ear while working at his latest project. His thick head of curly white hair would be bowed over, intent on the task at hand but never too busy to find the time to talk and share his wisdom.

At that moment, I bowed my own head and I asked Eugene to help me. I knew if anyone could help me in a somewhat mechanical situation, it would be him. I envisioned his twinkling gray-blue eyes—eyes full of life and love that were never too busy to help a friend.

I reached for the padlock and tried the key again. It moved! A chill went through my body as the key turned and the lock popped open in my hand. I stared in utter amazement at the padlock. I took the key out and stood there for a moment, trying to grasp the miracle that had just taken place. I looked up to the twinkling stars in sky and thanked Eugene.

I ran into the house, found Mom, and recounted the event that had just taken place. We went into the bedroom to check on Dad. He was feeling much better and sat up and listened to my story. He and Mom went out to the boat and examined the key and padlock. Dad asked me to put the key in and try it again. I told him I doubted it would work a second time. We'd experienced something quite unusual at a time when we most needed it. I inserted the key. I tried to turn it and it wouldn't budge. "Eugene's miracle," I said, looking at my parents.

Dad and I headed out for Tucson a few hours later. When I returned, I went to the pawnshop and related my story to Eugene's family. They were very moved by the event. There have been many times since then that I have asked Eugene for his help. It has always been a great comfort in my life to have my very own mechanically inclined guardian angel, especially one that I was fortunate enough to know at one time here on Earth.

—*Laura Ann Ostermeyer,*
Tucson, Ariz.

Poltergeist Activity

A poltergeist can be loosely described as a disembodied entity that manifests itself through creating chaos, making noises, moving objects, and, for all intents and purposes, disturbing the living. In German, the very word *poltern* means to "make noise" or "cause a racket," while *geist* quite simply means "ghost" or "specter." These entities are often drawn to negative energy and dysfunctional places and can sometimes be manifested by the living themselves due to an inability to reconcile internal qualms. Energy, not finding an outlet internally, sometimes externalizes and projects itself in terrifying, violent, and disturbing ways on the earth plane. Other times a poltergeist may be residual, occupying a home or place, terrorizing any-one who attempts to occupy its space.

Like a call from the universe to pay attention, poltergeists do whatever it takes to catch the interest of the living, usually performing their rotten deeds in random and unpredictable ways, raising the stress of the situation by leaps and bounds. Feeding off the fear of the tormented, these entities can quickly gain lever-age over the living in compounding order, making the very essence of their genesis the key to their survival. While not all poltergeists need be menacing—perhaps merely being entities that use noise and disorder to get the attention of the living—often the effects left in the wake of a poltergeist are undesirable and chaotic.

Popularized by American motion pictures, though certainly not originating in the box office, the idea of a poltergeist has captivated the imaginations of people for centuries and beyond. Here is but a taste of the horror, frustration, and sometimes mere disinterested wonderment that a handful of FATE readers have expe-rienced at the hands of such entities.

Tap-Tap-Tap

In 1961, I transferred to Chung-Kung Elementary School in Tainan, Taiwan. For the following two years (fifth and sixth grade), our class occupied the room at the west end of the second floor, right next to a wide stairway. The classroom was big and bright with windows on both south and north sides.

Back then, kids in elementary school in Tainan had to take a nap for 30 minutes after lunch. No exceptions. We sat at our desks, heads resting on our folded arms and eyes closed, while our teacher, Ms. Shu, walked between the rows. The "tap-tap-tap" of her high heels always told us where she was. From the paces and pauses between her footsteps, we could tell she was watching us.

On one particular day, I was not sleepy at all. The napping position soon became very uncomfortable. A short moment after Ms. Shu walked past my desk, I lifted my head, trying to stretch. To my surprise, I didn't see anyone at the spot where I thought Ms. Shu was. Puzzled, I looked around and found Ms. Shu napping at her own desk ten feet away from me in the northeast corner of the room.

Next day, the day after . . . every day, during our napping time, there was this "tap-tap-tap" going around the classroom—but no sight of the person who made the sound.

Teachers borrowed supplies (colored chalk, erasers, a stick for beating students) from each other once in a while. Usually, the teacher would send a student to the other classroom to do the borrowing. When the student arrived, he would say "Bao-Dao" (excuse me) to announce his presence at the door and then specify what he wanted to borrow. Several times I heard someone shout, "Bao-Dao," but when I looked up, no one was at the door.

In Taiwan, we often read aloud as a group. One day, Ms. Shu asked us to read a chapter out loud. In the middle of the reading, I heard Ms. Shu clap her hands and say, "Okay. That's enough." I stopped immediately. All my classmates stopped too. Ms. Shu looked confused. She asked, "Why do you stop? CONTINUE!"

Although I was not particularly scared of going to school every morning, I was terrified of being there after dark. One time Ms. Shu was mad at us for doing poorly in an academic competition, so she punished us by making us stay after school. As the minutes went by, and the room got darker, my heart pounded harder and harder. I thought we would all die in the classroom that night. When she finally let us go, everyone ran. No one wanted to be the last person to leave.

I had a recurring nightmare about that room. It would be dark outside and I would remember we had an exam on the next day. Unfortunately, I had left my book at the school. I begged my mom to get my book for me, but she said "no." My brother wouldn't either. The next thing I knew was I was at the bottom of the school stairway. I was scared and didn't want to go up.

"I am getting closer to my book," I thought. "I can do it!"

I knew I needed the book; I didn't have any choice. I would run up as fast as I could, with my eyes tightly shut. When I finally opened my eyes, I was in total darkness, the kind of darkness that had no respect for one's life. At that point, the dream always ended.

I had not discussed these strange things with any of my friends until several of us were invited to a birthday party. At the party, Feng-Xiang, the girl who sat in front of me in school, suddenly asked if any of us had noticed anything strange about the high-heel tapping sound during the nap time. One by one, we nodded.

"You know that it was not Ms. Shu, don't you? It's creepy!" She took a deep breath and continued, "We ought to do something about it. If we do it together, we will be okay." She looked around; nobody was willing to meet her eyes.

"Just talking about it gives me goosebumps all over," one girl said. We all laughed without wanting to.

"Next time, when I hear the footstep next to my desk, I am going to try to grab her," Feng-Xiang joked. Again, we laughed uneasily. None of us cared to say more. The conversation ended abruptly.

At the end of the year, we secretly congratulated each other for surviving "the room." I asked Feng-Xiang if she had tried to grab the invisible tapper like she said she would. She blinked her eyes and said, "Are you kidding? I am not stupid, am I?"

After all these years, every time I close my eyes, I hear that "tap-tap-tap."

—Helen Chen,
Rochester, Minn.

Who Was Driving the Car?

I was 76 years old when we moved to Leesburg, Florida. We bought a home like we'd always dreamed about, then settled down to enjoy our retirement. Between my pension and Social Security income, we were able to live comfortably, until expenses skyrocketed due to major medical bills for my wife and me, making it necessary to find some extra income.

Eventually I found work at a large grocery store as a bagger. My working hours were normally from 11:00 a.m. to 7:30 p.m. Driving home from work, I took Highway 441 to a small country road called Sleepy Hollow Road, about three or four miles long, that intersects with another country road called Sunny Side. Five days a week I drove home on Sleepy Hollow Road. As the days darkened, with no light of any sort on the road, the huge trees along both sides meeting above the road made me feel like I was driving through a tunnel.

This particular night, I was rather tired. There were small pockets of fog forming on the road, causing me to strain to see clearly and lowering my speed to 25 miles per hour. There were no cars in sight in either direction, and I was anxious to get home and have something to eat.

Sleepy Hollow Road is straight as an arrow. I don't understand what happened; I only recall that I suddenly realized I was traveling over 65 miles per hour, my hands and arms rigid, gripping the steering wheel as hard as possible. For some reason I did not or could not slow down.

Suddenly there was a brilliant flash of light inside my car (not lightning), snapping me out of my trance like a slap in the face. But I was still speeding directly toward the end of the road, where a big yellow and black triangular road sign stood with arrows pointing left and right. I do not remember slamming on my brakes, only staring horrified at the huge tree behind the yellow sign and hearing the screech of my tires as it seemed I was about to crash.

My car came to a stop just inches away from the post. My heart was beating a thousand times a minute, I was shaking all over from fright, and my hands were still gripping the steering wheel. When I managed to get out of the car, I saw the bumper was barely touching the signpost. I got back in the car, still shaking and too nervous to drive, then thanked the Lord for saving my life, finally driving slowly to my home.

I still drive Sleepy Hollow Road four or more times a week, but very, very carefully. The Lord or my guardian angel saved my life, of this I am certain. I do not know who, or if anyone, had anything to do with what happened. I am grateful for still being alive. It is a wonderful feeling believing someone is riding on my shoulder looking out for me.

—*Daniel Tarry,*
Leesburg, Fla.

Be Careful What You Say to Spirits

In 1994, I wrote about an unusual event that I experienced in 1991—"The Last Goodbye"—which was published in the November 1994 issue of FATE.

I had related the story of a neighbor whom I had befriended and who had died. The night after her death, a humming noise in the armoire next to my bed awakened me. It sounded like the hangers were rattling. At 7:30 the next morning, a faint double-ring sounded on the telephone. These beeps continued for several months at the exact same time. Eventually they stopped . . . and I wrote my letter to you.

I thought that was the end of it. However, after some time passed, the beeps returned, now always at 11:30 p.m. I grew used to the little "beep-beeps" and ignored them.

After they continued for some time, I began to consider the possibility that some exterior electrical event, moisture on the wires, or some other physical phenomenon was causing the beeping. I also considered the possibility that since the beeps occurred at the same time—and I expected them at that time—that my own energy force or psychic energy was causing the bells to chime. I discounted this, however, since many times I was asleep and awakened by the beeps.

I replaced all the wiring and connectors that led to the telephone, and still the beeps occurred—always at 11:30 p.m., despite time changes in the fall and spring.

One night, I was reading—and not paying any attention to the time—when the usual soft beep-beep occurred. I don't know why, but I said: "Is that the best you can do?"

The next night at exactly 11:30, a horrific bang sounded in the corner between the armoire and my bed. Terrified, I turned on the light to see what had happened. Nothing was amiss.

I said aloud: "Please don't ever do that again. You scared me."

The next night before retiring, I repeated my request. At 11:30, barely audible, the frailest "beep-beep" sounded. . . never to be heard again.

—Dorothy Marie,
Pleasant Hill, Calif.

A Mighty Restless Spirit

In 1990, Wilburn Heath purchased a couple of acres on the outskirts of Scottsboro. The area was quiet and seemed to be an ideal retirement site. He and Nina, his wife of 30 years, were making plans for their "laid back" years, which would be coming in the near future. Wilburn immediately began building the small, compact house that they both had agreed upon. It was at the stage that it could be lived in, but was lacking the finishing touches and trim work. He had completed a very large building that he intended to use for storage and for a workshop. After retirement, he planned to do some small jobs just to keep from getting bored. Wilburn was a mechanic by trade and had a habit of trading for junk car parts. He had hauled in loads of these items to the point that the lots were overflowing.

Right in the midst of their preparation for retirement, Nina was diagnosed with breast cancer. Although she fought a hard battle, she was taken from him within six months. Wilburn was devastated and attempted to bury himself in work. The thought of life without her was just unbearable. The long hours and mental anguish were taking their toll on his system.

But Wilburn didn't appear to have noticed except he had decided that he could not bear to live at that site. Wilburn approached his young nephew with an offer to sell the property to him. Steve was 23 years old and had a wife to be responsible for. He did have a good job with Current Electrical Co. However, he was not ready to make the major purchase of a house.

Steve gave the idea full consideration, then went back to talk to his uncle. He felt that with the house not being finished and the lots overflowing with junk, his chances of floating a loan were slim. He told Wilburn that he was willing to purchase the property, for the stated amount, providing that he be allowed to live on the property until it was in a more presentable condition. In lieu of rent, he would put the finishing touches on the house and clear away all the junk. A gentleman's agreement was reached, and, Steve and Karen moved into the house.

Right away, this young couple set about to complete the needed tasks. Quite naturally, they were very excited. It was a dream come true! They spent every spare moment in attempt to hasten things along. As each piece of trim was nailed and each load of junk was hauled away, their dream seemed to be moving closer. The quiet neighborhood would be ideal for the family they planned to have someday. Everything appeared to be falling into place nicely and the future looked bright Then, without prior warning, Wilburn was smitten with a fatal heart attack. Steve and Karen met with Nina's sister and her husband, who were attempting to put Wilburn's affairs in order. All were in agreement that the method of purchase that Wilburn had established with Steve was valid and should stand as it was.

Both the house and lot were showing a marked improvement. Steve and Karen felt that within a couple of months they would be ready to secure a loan and finalize all the necessary paperwork. But suddenly, strange things began to happen. Porcelain figurines came flying through the air and crashed against walls. Appliances stopped working for no apparent reason. Bad luck of all kinds was engulfing them. They tried to stay optimistic by telling each other that it was the strain of the situation. Such things can't happen. But the worst was yet to come. Their doorbell began to ring at late hours of the night. Whenever Steve went to check, no one was anywhere around. Being an electrician, Steve felt that was a small problem. Somehow, the wiring must have gotten a short. He took care of the problem by disconnecting the doorbell until he had time to properly rewire it.

With that problem taken care of, they settled in for a peaceful night. It was a major shock when the doorbell continued to ring at wee hours of the night. The whole situation was beginning to grate their nerves. Soon, they felt that something had to be done. Since we all know that such things can't happen, they determined that they must be imagining part of this. They decided to go out and shop for a loan on Steve's next day off from work. They were sure that once they had gotten everything into legal order, they would be more relaxed and the nonsense would stop.

The following day when Steve arrived home, Karen was visibly shaken. She told her husband that she had started into the bedroom to do some cleaning, but a man was standing in the doorway blocking her way. She went on to say that he just stood there, looking at her, then disappeared from sight. In answer to Steve's questions, she described this mysterious figure as being about six-feet, one-inch tall and stout. He had blond hair with a crew cut. His eyes were clear blue and piercing. Steve swallowed hard and said, "Uncle Wilburn!"

The following day, Steve had a day off from work. So he and Karen headed for Scottsboro in search of a loan. Their hopes were soon shattered. Neither bank nor finance company would grant the needed loan. Disappointment was overwhelming. They had worked so hard. For what?

Within a short period of time, this young couple had located another place, and had no problem with securing a loan. As they engaged in packing and moving things out, everything began to calm down. Once they had gotten settled into their new home, everything was quiet and peaceful. There were no weird noises or flying objects.

In summing up this story, Steve said, "I always liked Uncle Wilburn, I wouldn't have minded to have helped, had he still been alive. But I still wonder why his spirit was so restless."

—Mary R. Crawford,
Dutton, Ala.

Mysteries

When I lived in New York City during the early to mid-1960s, I often noticed a tiny flat black square, perhaps twice the size of the period at the end of this sentence, embedded in the "webby" area between the thumb and index finger of my left hand. Sometimes it was there and sometimes it wasn't. If you spread your fingers and hold your hand up to the light, you can see through the skin in that area. While I often wondered what it was, I haven't seen it for years. While such things didn't exist during that time period, I realized some years ago that it resembled a tiny computer chip.

During the mid-1970s, I was living in a luxury high-rise apartment building right behind Grauman's Chinese Theatre in Hollywood. After stepping out of the shower one afternoon, I noticed something red on the towel I was using to dry my face with. I held the towel open and saw a large handprint that appeared to be the size of an adult male hand with the fingers spread widely apart. It appeared to be dried blood. I thought, *My God, am I bleeding?*

I searched every part of my body, and the towel and bath mat, both of which were white, and could not find a trace of fresh blood anywhere. It took several washings with bleach before that handprint disappeared from the towel.

During the early 1980s, still living in the same building, but in an apartment on a higher floor, I had what I believe was a dream, although to this day I'm not sure whether it was a dream or not. I found myself standing in my bedroom, facing the window wall, which looked down on Franklin Avenue and the Magic Castle, a legendary hangout for magicians, and Yamashiro, the Japanese restaurant on the hill above it.

The only difference was that the bedroom wall had disappeared, and I was looking up at the night sky. From the northeast, a colossal cross, which appeared to be made of a silvery-colored metal, bearing an equally enormous figure of Christ, descended slowly from the night sky. Looking like something Salvador Dali would have created, this spectacular crucifix was surrounded by angels, and was accompanied by music that was beautiful beyond anything I have ever heard.

A year or so later, in that same bedroom, I had a near-death experience. I found myself flying, accompanied by another entity. Eventually, I arrived at a place where the only thing I saw was a narrow but tremendously tall Gothic door. There were other entities there. We communicated telepathically. I was told that I could go through the door or return to 1746 N. Orange Drive; the choice was mine. If I chose to pass through the door, there would be no returning until I decided to reincarnate again. I did think about it for a while, as I was in really bad pain from arthritis in my shoulder.

Suddenly I heard, as if from a great distance, my poodle Mr. Tuffy barking. I loved him just as much as I loved Bruce, who had been my companion for five years. I had no idea then how much Bruce would need me in later years, but I felt that Mr. Tuffy was calling me back for a reason. As soon as I decided to go back, I felt myself falling back into my body, and immediately felt the pain in my shoulder. I rose out of, and fell back into, my body five or six times before I felt permanently locked in.

During the 1990s, we were living in Las Vegas. Bruce had been diagnosed with full-blown AIDS in

1992, when we lived in Ft. Lauderdale. On the day of the next strange occurrence, he was in Canada, visiting his family. This was during the summer of 1995. I had taken Scarlett O'Hara, our Yorkie, who was Mr. Tuffy's successor, out for a walk. We were in the complex, which was a walled and gated townhouse community. No one could enter or leave without inserting a card at the gate, and I knew most of the tenants. An adults-only community, no one under the age of 50 lived there.

After walking for a few minutes, I saw a beautiful young blond woman in pink shorts and a white top approaching us on a bicycle. She stopped next to where we were standing and reached down to pet Scarlett, and called her by her name. Raising her head, she looked me straight in the eye. "Bruce's pain and suffering will soon be over. You will be here with him until the end. You have many years left. May God be with you." Scarlett tugged on her leash, distracting me for a moment. When I turned back around just an instant later, the lady on the bicycle was gone. From where we were standing, she would have had to pedal at least a block to have disappeared.

Well, I thought to myself, in Las Vegas in the summer, I guess even angels wear shorts.

Bruce left this plane two years later. Before he left on his celestial journey, I said to him, "Honey, I know you're going to want to take a long rest, but when you have time, please come around and let us know that you're okay." He had been seeing his mother near his bed during those final days. Four months to the day after she took his hand and led him to another world out there, Scarlett and I moved to Tennessee.

I haven't seen Bruce, but I often feel his presence. He loved to gamble as much as I do, and every time I've gone to Harrah's Casino in Cherokee, North Carolina, I know he has been in the car with me. My sister Millie, who adored Bruce, once saw him in her apartment in Hollywood, standing in her kitchen door with his arms folded. He smiled at her and then disappeared.

I always read before going to sleep. I lay the book or magazine on the floor next to my bed, lie on my stomach, and hang my head over the side of the bed. For at least three decades, after turning off the light, I continue reading. The room is dark, my eyes are closed, but I can see perfectly. Instead of *Newsweek* or Stephen King, I'm now reading a scroll, which is unrolling slowly. I can hear myself reading aloud, though the scroll appears to be written in Hebrew—a language I don't understand.

For some reason, I've always been able to feel other people's pain, and it isn't pleasant. The worst is those people who seem to relish telling about their surgeries. When they begin describing where the surgeon made an incision or sutured a wound, I feel the pain so intently in that spot that I'm in agony, and have to cut them off abruptly. I described this problem to a psychic once. She said I had the ability to be a healer.

A few nights ago, I woke up about three in the morning, colder than I have ever been in my life. The heat was on, and my bedroom was warm enough that before turning the light off, I had kicked the covers off. I was literally freezing. My teeth were chattering and my whole body was shaking violently. Somehow, I managed to get out of bed and put on some socks and a heavy bathrobe. I grabbed more blankets and got back into bed. Curling into a fetal position, I lay there for about an hour before the trembling subsided. When this frightening episode was over, the bedroom was still nice and warm, and again I kicked off the covers.

This same thing occurred a couple of years ago, although not nearly as severe. I was so exhausted, I went back to bed and slept all afternoon. I called my doctor and told her what happened. She didn't have a clue. Somehow, I couldn't bring myself to tell her that it was as if I had been in the icy depths of outer space.

Could it be that I was perhaps experiencing the suffering of someone a world away, taking some of the cold away from them, and preventing them from freezing to death?

If any of FATE's enlightened readers can help me solve even a few of these bizarre mysteries, and perhaps tell me why these things are happening to me, I shall be eternally grateful.

—*Donald Taylor,*
Johnson City, Tenn.

Living with Spirits

Since I was a child a feeling of ice cold going over me has happened quite regularly. There was never an explanation for this, only that it might be a draft. At the age of 17, I was thrown into a pool by a group of boys playing around. Going under the water several times, life passed by me quickly and everything went dark. A face appeared to me that I did not recognize. A feeling of being lifted toward the surface of the water made my body feel strange, but the face was still with me. After that I remember lying on the riverbank with people standing over me. A young man had jumped in and dragged me from the edge of the pool. Recovering from my ordeal, I asked him about the other person in the water, but he said there was no one else. From that day, through illness or bad times, someone has always been near, touching me and stroking my face. I am convinced that a spirit (or maybe more than one) is with me.

A recent tragedy in the family took the life of a young boy, only 22 years old. He was my nephew who I loved very much. Sometimes there is a feeling of his presence when it is quiet, or I am alone in the house. Living with spirits is not frightening once you have got used to them.

One night I was awakened by the sound of a little girl singing and my wind chimes jingling. My husband got out of bed, looked around all the bedrooms, but could not find anyone. He blamed it on the wind, but a feeling inside me knew different. A howling noise like a wolf was heard on a couple of occasions coming from my youngest daughter's bedroom. This was very weird, but again nothing could be found, only my daughter sleeping soundly.

Family and friends come to the house most days visiting. They have gotten used to the noises by now—creaking stairs, a kettle that turns on and off on its own, or the jukebox playing records. They used to cringe at the thought of spirits being around them, but it has not stopped them from visiting me and my family. Our house is over 100 years old and once upon a time was owned by a farmer. The house was then made of old stone. Two walls have remained the same, but a great deal of renovation has been done over the years to the inside; extensions have made the house a lot bigger than when it was first built. It is known that people have passed away in our house, some I knew as a child, the last one being a lovely and respectable man who passed away only five years ago. My family and I moved into the house a few months later.

There was a eerie feeling to the house from the moment I stepped through the door. This soon passed once I was settled in. The once dark and dull walls are now brightly colored. A log fire on cold winter nights makes the house feel warm and cozy. Next to the fireplace is an alcove. A cupboard was built into this over

50 years ago. At night when we are watched televi-sion, the doors open with a bang hitting against the wall.

Strange noises can be heard in a lot of homes. Some have a logical explanation; others do not. In my home there must be a lot of old memories, some sad and I am sure some happy ones too. I am convinced there are spirits here. Some people think this is all in my mind, and that I am a little eccentric.

Seeing is believing. I know the face in the pool saved me from a tragic end. I hope the spirits will guide me through the rest of my life.

—*Carol Walker,*
Long Bennington, England

Sandi's Dream House

As my friend Walter Janin and I lugged the heavy Duncan Phyffe table from the dining room into the living room, there was a thunderous pounding on the front door. The banging continued with a sense of urgency, but when I opened the door, there was no one there.

As I questioned my senses, Walter confirmed that he too had heard the noise, but couldn't explain it. He was selling the table and chairs and I was helping him get ready to put the house up for sale.

Later that night, stranger things happened. As I lay in bed, I heard Walter walking down the hall, but never saw him pass my doorway. I got up to find him asleep in the den, TV on, at the opposite end of the house.

The next morning, I was surprised to find the new dining room table laden with votive candles, a Bible, a statue of Mary, a rosary, and a crucifix. It was a touching, almost childlike display, the way a youngster would gather up makeshift weapons for protection.

"All hell broke loose in here last night," Walter said, entering the room. He said he had gotten up several times to check the front door, hearing it opening and closing. When he settled back down, almost asleep, a ghostly figure swept by him, went to the window, and drew the curtain aside. He was later awakened by the clattering of lids on the crocks in the living room. They were heavy old clay pickle barrels, not prone to vibrations.

What was going on? Neither of us had ever encountered anything supernatural, and we were like kids trying to decipher the plot of a bad horror movie. We were nervous, especially me, since I didn't know Walter that well. I had just met him several months prior, shortly after his wife Sandi had died.

According to Walter, Sandi proposed to him within hours after they met. Walter was a Croatian immigrant, recently divorced after a 35-year marriage. She was lonely. He was lonely. She wasted no time convincing him to marry her and move to Florida from Mansfield, Ohio. She brought her precious antiques and an enviable collection of early American pottery, now being sold. I found a list of all her treasured items, along with diagrams of the rooms, showing where each piece was to go.

When the newlyweds arrived in Inglis, Florida, Sandi said she didn't feel well and asked to go to Seven Rivers Hospital in Crystal River. Doctors there sadly advised her that she had about 30 days to live. Cancer, thought to be in remission, now consumed her. Devastated and in denial, Walter and Sandi returned immediately to Ohio. Sandi died 23 days later. She never spent one night in her dream home.

I had the uneasy feeling that Sandi's spirit didn't approve of our alterations. I suggested disposing of her personal items immediately, hoping that would sever her attachment to the house, if she was indeed responsible for the haunting. Assuring Walter all would go to a good cause, I promised to donate everything to Goodwill. From her hope chest came a wedding dress, a moth-eaten mink collar, slips, veil, gloves, and on and on. Walter could barely close the drawstring on the plastic bag, which he placed in my Toyota.

As I backed out of the garage, the automatic door came down heavily on the trunk with a crushing sound. I leaped out to inspect the damage, but thankfully, it bounced up as soon as it hit. To my surprise, Walter was standing alongside the driveway with the remote in his hand, grinning, his eyes glazed. I got goosebumps looking at him, unable to believe he was responsible for such a dumb act.

"You idiot!" I screamed. "Are you trying to wreck my car?"

In a woman's voice, he promised not to do it again, saying he was just trying to be funny. Backing out quickly, I sped east, clutching the steering wheel so tight that my hands got cramps, expecting some demonic force to yank it away and cause me to crash into a tree. I strained to look into every oncoming car, checking for a driver with horns and eyes that gleamed like fire. I threw the bag into the first dumpster I spotted, breathing a sigh of relief.

As we weren't finished redecorating, I agreed to return the following weekend and headed for my condo in St. Pete, glad to be leaving.

Night after night, I got calls from Walter. The presence had taken up a position in the den, and loud scratching and clawing noises came from inside the wall. He had the house blessed by the parish priest. Having it consecrated made him feel better, but the noises continued. Fortunately, it soon sold, and Walter moved to Bushnell, Florida.

Did Sandi's spirit remain in her dream house? Did it move with Walter to Bushnell? Does a spirit eventually lose its energy and dissipate? Is Sandi now at peace? I hope so.

—*Pat Scanlon,*
St. Petersburg, Fla.

9

Astral Phenomenon, Vortexes, and Space-Time Slips

The philosopher Plato first noted the astral plane as the place within which the eternal form of everything exists beyond the physical realm. It is often known as the "subtle" part of the being that can transcend imposed space-time boundaries and visit the edges of the universe, otherwise unreachable in the physical body. Nonetheless, the idea of reincarnation and a sort of "underworld"—a place where someone would eventually go without their body—is nothing new to the world. Shamanism, for instance, is the practice of peeling back the layers of the eternal, or Spirit World, while both Egyptians and Tibetans account for intermediate worlds beyond the Earth—the Duat and the Bardo, respectively. Christianity, of course, has Heaven and Hell while Buddhism has Nirvana (and the list goes on).

There is something to be said for the consistent recognition of astral possibilities across peoples and cultures throughout time. While, of course, every one of these cultures has their own nuances differentiating each from the other, one must look into the epistemological value of mankind's numerous recognitions of a world beyond.

If indeed these realms do exist, could all cultures be looking into the same reality and giving it a different name? And if so, does the living Earth have to die before visiting such a plane?

This chapter relates to stories occupying and exploring the astral body without putting to death the physical being. While not all of the stories deal with astral projection, nearly every story calls into question the true nature of time and existence. Can one entity be in two places at once? You be the judge.

He Did it to Me Again

The story "Who's Been Walking on My Bed?" about my husband (Richard) going on an astral walkabout from his body and totally freaking me out was published in the August 2001 issue of Fate. Well, dear readers, he did it to me again!

In the early morning hours of October 6, 2002, something woke me up. The room just didn't feel right. As I opened my eyes, I saw my somnolent husband white as a sheet, with dark caverns under his eyes, standing motionless in the pitch-black recesses of the closet staring at me. Like in the first story, Richard had been sleeping on the couch, only this time we were both ill. While we both suffered from fevers, I had the chills, so I was piled with blankets, which to him felt suffocating, so he'd opted for the couch. A quick glance around the bedroom told me that the hallway door was still closed. If he had opened it, I would have awakened. Combine this with the fact that I had been to a funeral the previous day, and naturally I concluded that he had died.

I started screaming. My heart was racing, but I managed to throw my hand out and hit the touch lamp. The light caused his ghostly image to vanish. It took me a couple of minutes to recover enough to fight my way out of the tangled covers. By the time I got into the hallway, Richard was stumbling toward the bedroom.

"Was that you screaming?" he asked. It must be very disorienting to be slapped back into your body so suddenly.

"Yes!"

I was furious with him. I don't know why he always visits me when he takes a trip out of his body. One day he's going to scare me out of mine for keeps! We live in a high-rise apartment building. Why can't he go stare at the neighbors while they're sleeping? I can see the odd looks of recognition he would get on the elevator already!

—*Kelly Steed,*
Harrison Township, Mich.

From a Bird's Eye View

We seldom went to the doctor when I was growing up. Mother and Grandma tended to our ailments with "those wonderful home remedies." Usually, these took care of the problem—or, at least, discouraged us from complaining.

No one in our immediate family had ever been admitted to a hospital. I did have a first cousin who had an appendectomy when I was quite young. However, I had never been inside a hospital until I was 14.

As luck would have it, about three and a half months after I turned 14, I was smitten with an acute attack of appendicitis. Our family doctor recommended surgery ASAP. Despite my protests, I was admitted to the hospital early the next morning.

Needless to say, I was petrified with fear. To make bad matters worse, a nurse came and took away all my clothes, including my underwear. This was the pits of humiliation. There I was in a strange place, among strange people, and practically naked. No matter how hard I begged for my underwear, the nurse kept refusing to give them to me.

After an hour or so, I was wheeled away for surgery. This was in the good old days, so I was put under with ether. When they placed the mask over my face and told me to breathe deeply so that I would be nicely asleep, I wanted to jump up and run away.

Then, I could feel myself rising to the ceiling of the operating room. Soon, I could see everything that was happening down there. My body was having its appendix taken out. Strangely enough, I didn't care because I wasn't in my body, and I knew that they weren't hurting me.

After the surgery was completed, and they were covering my body with a blanket, somehow I was back in it and was wheeled back to my room to recover.

The nurse, who assisted with the operation, was shocked when I repeated everything that had taken place or had been discussed during the surgery. I did not talk about this for many years, for fear of being ridiculed, but I did tell Mother while I was recovering. She told me that I was just imagining this because

I was asleep and could not have seen nor heard anything. However, I always knew better.

This story is true. As I look back to the circumstances surrounding this incident, I believe that I was scared right out of my body. It simply was my way of dealing with a horrifying experience from which I could not escape.

—Mary R. Crawford,
Dutton, Ala.

Like Father, Like Daughter

When I was 13 years old, my family moved from a town in New Mexico to a small farm community in Oklahoma. In the early fall in Oklahoma, the evenings were pleasant, with balmy breezes having a hypnotic quality. Accordingly, the bed in my new bedroom was placed directly under a window in order to take advantage of the fresh night air.

One evening, I lay in bed waiting to drift off to sleep. The house was still. The night was pleasant, with a gentle breeze. I was on top of the bedspread, half-awake, slipping into sleep. I began to hum at first and then to sing softly a little Spanish song I had learned at school in New Mexico. I focused my attention on the evening's serenity, the feel of the soothing light wind whispering over me, and the smell of the pristine night air.

Then, effortlessly I left my body, conscious of lying prone but at the same time wafting like smoke up into the air. This was the greatest feeling of peace that I had ever known. Yet, as I was enjoying the sensation of freedom, the reality of my situation seeped into my awareness. I suddenly became frightened, took in a gasping breath, and felt myself falling, as if physically returning to my body with an audible "plop."

I had never heard of out-of-body experiences. At the time, the concept was foreign to me and completely disconcerting. It would be years before I shared this incident with anyone. When I finally told the tale, it was to my mother, who related a story to me about my dad, who had passed on years before.

It seems that when Mother and Dad first married, he told Mother that he sometimes dreamed of leaving his body. When this occurred and he became aware of his state, he immediately attempted to re-enter the body, which would result in uncontrollable shaking. This condition was unpleasant to him and he told Mother if she ever noticed him trembling in his sleep, to awaken him in order to put a stop to the incident.

Sure enough, one evening Mother awoke to Dad shaking violently. Following his request, she carefully nudged him. When fully awake, he told her that he had indeed left his body, floating out the bedroom window and down to an apartment where another young married couple resided. He observed the pair in the midst of a serious quarrel having something to do with the husband's parents. Viewing the argument was upsetting to him, and he was grateful to return to his body.

Later the next morning, after Dad left for work, Mother had an unexpected visit from the young wife whom Dad had reported seeing. She was upset, crying, and spoke to Mother about an argument she and her husband had in the middle of the night. It seems they were in disagreement about a visit from his parents. The neighbor's report coincided in every detail to Dad's story, confirming the veracity of the incident to Mother. Although Mother comforted her, she did not tell the young woman about Dad's experience.

Since my initial experience, I have undergone other similar events. This leads me to pose the question: Why do some people experience this while others do not? Perhaps the answer lies in heredity. Some people have blue eyes, as do their parents. Some people have red hair. Some people are predisposed to out-of-body experiences. Maybe it really is in the genes!

—*Donetta Briody,*
Punta Gorda, Fla.

Nearby Realities

I was looking away when Michael ran past, but turned around when he cried in pain. By then he was holding onto his wrist, which hung at a sickening angle. It was a terrible sight, but I summoned composure and wrapped my calm around the child. The biggest problem was communication. I couldn't leave him alone, so I sent his friend Khalid to the office for assistance.

Time seemed suspended where Michael and I sat waiting for help to come. Other students ran wildly nearby on the playground as if he and I were invisible. He pressed his forehead against my leg and stayed quiet after he first cried out. Too quiet, and a little shocky.

Inside my head, one thought recurred: Call 911! It quieted when Khalid returned with Sally, the school health aide.

I felt relieved and watched through the window as Michael walked away with Sally and Jim, our expert in child development. Jim naturally inspired confidence in emergencies. He reminded me so much of my late father, a veteran firefighter who was first on the scene in a crisis.

Dad—Capt. Roy Swenson—had been killed two years earlier while responding to an accident on the interstate. My parents divorced when I was young, and I hadn't talked to Dad in the years before his death. In many ways, I felt closer to him afterward, as if we could better understand each other outside the limits of space and time.

The school was near his old station house. Inspection tags on the classroom extinguishers still carried his stamp: "Checked by R. Swenson." I thought of him often, and more than once, I'd noticed how much Jim was like him, the way they walked and carried themselves, the way they took charge of tough situations.

I truly believed Michael was in the care of the two most qualified people in school—until the Monday morning after the accident, when Sally stopped by the teachers' lounge and asked if I wanted to talk.

"My impulse," I confided nervously, "was to call 911."

"I've been wondering about that too," said Sally, "but everything worked out in the end. Michael's father arrived within minutes."

"Jim didn't suggest a call either, right? He assessed the situation the same as you?"

For a moment, she looked confused while she considered the events of that day.

"Jim wasn't with us," she said with certainty. "Nobody was." Then she studied my face as my mind briefly lurched and made an unsuccessful grab at the tangible.

I plainly remembered looking through the window as the three of them walked to the office. I saw Sally on Michael's left and Jim on his right, but from behind, I had mixed up my heroes.

A few years back, there was a *Nova* episode about time travel. It suggested an infinite number of timelines that mirrored our infinite choices. Some realities would be vastly divergent. Others would be much closer to waking life and occasionally intersecting.

I'd needed a hero, and in a nearby reality, Dad answered my call to 911.

—*Tina Dybvik,*
Saint Paul, Minn.

Awakenings

As I stooped and went through the heavy wooden doors, I said to myself, "I am home." As I write about this unique event, I feel my spine crawl and I become emotional, even today, long after I walked through these magnificent doors. I had never in my days and all my travels around the world said this, but here I knew something special.

As I walked through the great Cathedral of Rheims (90 kilometers east of Paris, France), I put my initial feelings out of my mind as I photographed the spectacular stained-glass windows, ceilings, and huge pillars.

Later, I returned to find a Mass starting and went in, even though I knew the entire service would be in French, a language of limited expertise with me. As I stood there facing the altar and the magnificent windows, tears started rolling down my eyes. My body was all "tingly." I tried to cover up these feelings, but throughout the entire service, my soul had a major experience.

In a vision, I saw the doors open, and watched a very important individual coming in to be crowned—as 25 kings and an emperor were in this great cathedral. I saw crowds, but my focus was on the person coming in. I realized that I was re-experiencing my participation in a long-ago ceremony. I was someone with important military responsibilities, and I was at this ceremony because I had earned it in service to the leader coming in to be crowned.

The experience of reliving a past-life memory was a major reinforcement of my philosophical understanding. I had not sought this or expected this during my 35 days in France. I never thought about it. Yet it happened and the event was so moving that anytime I share it, my whole body reacts strongly. This was a major soul-life experience.

I have experienced three similar events in my time, but none was so traumatic as this one. I had one spine-tingling event when I stood in Chichen Itza by the great Pyramid. The other two experiences relate directly to Rheims.

Years ago, I walked through Versailles, the grand palace of the French kings. As I walked to the front door, I felt I had done this before. Later, when I walked into a yellow, administrative-looking room, the spine tingles occurred very strongly. Another time, while riding in Paris, I had those overwhelming feelings again. As I looked at the map, I discovered that we were at the location of the famous Bastille prison.

In trying to piece these experiences together, I remembered a regression situation where I had gone back in time and saw myself suddenly riding on a horse, in full military officer attire, in a major battle. Looking across a little hill, I saw a great leader on his horse. It was Napoleon. I suspect that this was the famous battle of Austerlitz, but I have no proof. I have done research on Napoleon's campaigns and battles to see if anything came through the memory-fog of life, but no names or situations seem to answer.

I felt certain at one time that the leader I saw coming through the door at Rheims was Napoleon, and that I was an officer working for him. But it could have been any of the monarchs who were crowned at Rheims and administered at Versailles.

Sometimes memories return from nowhere, without any expectation. Sometimes the emotions are so strong that one knows this was an important memory from the past. The past helps us understand who we are and why we are. It explains strong interests and skills, as well as problems and concerns developed in this lifetime. The key is to be alert for signs from one's soul.

The past is past; the only day that counts is today, but we can and must learn from our past.

—Dr. Ron Anjard,
San Diego, Calif.

Soul Retrieval

There is an endless supply of metaphysical books available. There is also an increasing belief in and use of spirit guides. There are many confusing definitions of spirit guides, bordering on and overlapping with angels. In a desire to be part of this New Age "in crowd," more people openly admit—and even brag about—contacting the spiritual realm for guidance.

As with the American psyche in general, more is better. One person I met announced he had 44 spirit guides. In some cases, they become like an addiction. People ask their spirit guides about decisions to be made. Guides are implored to watch over families and keep them safe—sometimes even to find someone a parking place.

My story and painting, simply put, are about using the spirits of dead people to guide the living. Somehow, the belief has sprung up that because spirits are dead, they suddenly have an incredible amount of information. It doesn't occur to people that, perhaps, the way the spirits were when they had a body is continued into the afterlife—that they may still have limitations and wishes of their own. People assume that the departed don't mind being interrupted on their spiritual journey—that they're ready and waiting to give vacation tips or decide where to go for lunch.

A friend of mine bought a book and did a great job of learning how to find and use spirits of Native Americans and a totem animal—a crow—to do her bidding. She proudly asked me to look at what she was doing because I am a psychic.

My friend had followed the book's instructions to a T. She even bought a leather bag in which to keep her ceremonial items. She had successfully made contact with five Native American spirits who had been massacred by white men. In all the confusion of trying to avoid being killed by fire or shot, to find and save their loved ones, to find an escape route, the shock was too overwhelming: They did not pass in peace. They were stuck in a state of unrest. They wanted to be found, but not by a white woman who just wanted to use them.

When I communicated with these spirits about what they needed, their shaman appeared. He had been present at the time of the massacre, but he could only help so many of his people. Others had been lost in the shuffle of mass murder and mayhem.

What I saw, clairvoyantly, was the medicine man standing on a hill overlooking the destruction of his village. He wore a pouch on his side. He sent off the crow to find the departed souls and bring them to him for a spiritual healing, so they could go on and take their next step on the spiritual path. His people were very relieved to be free of my friend.

Sure, you can work with spirit guides, but should you? Can you tell the difference between an angel and dead person? You must take into account that some of these spirit guides are earthbound dead people. They had bodies and experiences just like you and me. Whatever happened to the old saying, "Do unto others as you would have them do unto you"?

Just imagine for a moment that you have passed on and strangers keep asking you to do this, that, and the other for them. Worse yet, imagine you're the spirit of a Native American, whose culture and people have been nearly wiped out by the white man. Still, that wasn't enough: They use your drums and chants, your sweat lodges and rituals—and now, they even want your soul!

—*Ria Ritka,*
Aurora, Colo.

Stop Steering

Several years ago, the word "psychic" meant very little to me; the word "medium" meant even less. I worked as a counselor at a shelter for abused women and children. This position required that I work midnight shifts on a regular basis. My workplace was about 30 miles from my home. Sometimes in the winter it felt like I was taking my life in my own hands just traveling back and forth on the highway. I was a very nervous winter driver. By the time I had completed the 40-minute drive to work, I would usually have had at least four cigarettes just to keep my nerves calm.

On this particular occasion, I had borrowed my boyfriend's car, as mine was having trouble starting. I always felt that my own car was better in the snow, but I settled for his as I was in a pinch. The drive to work that night wasn't too bad, but still I was very nervous because something unusual had happened before I left home.

As was my habit, I was lying in bed, trying to get some rest. I had to stay awake all night on my shift. When I went to lie down I happened to glance out my front door and noticed that it was starting to snow. *Oh no*, I thought. I went upstairs and tried to settle down. Finally my mind started to relax and I wondered to myself what the drive would be like coming home.

Within a few seconds of posing this question, I had what I now know to be a vision. As clear as anything you could ever watch on television, I saw myself spinning in circles on the highway. I can barely describe the terror I felt. It was so real. The vision lasted a few seconds and then stopped. I shook my head feeling stunned. What was that? I had never experienced anything like it in my life.

After that I knew I couldn't settle down, so I got up and made myself a cup of coffee. I had this overwhelming feeling that I should call in to work and tell them I couldn't make it. But what could I say? "Look, I'm sorry but I can't make it in. I had a vision that if I drove to work I would end up losing control of my car on the highway"? I sat and shook for a few minutes, trying to figure out what to do. Finally I decided to muster up my courage and drive to work.

The roads were starting to get slippery, but I made it in. However, when I left for home in the morning, the roads were much worse. I barely made it out of town, almost side-swiping an ambulance and a fire truck that were stopped because of a bad accident. I got to the highway and decided it was much too slippery to drive all the way home. My thought was to drive to the garage up the road and then call home for a ride.

But I didn't make it that far. I couldn't have gotten more than several hundred feet down the road when I lost control of the car. It started to spin in circles, first one way and then the other. I was horrified. I knew that if I didn't get the car off the road it was only a matter of time before another car came along and hit me. All at once, I felt like I was finished. I was going to die. I said a prayer asking God that if I was meant to die to not let it be painful.

I prayed very hard and suddenly, the car seemed to fill up with light, to the point that I could no longer see out the windows. I know this sounds unbelievable, but as the car filled with light, I heard a voice say: "Stop steering."

For some reason, without thinking about why I was hearing such a voice, I replied: "I can't; I've got to get off the road."

I tried a few more times, and the car just kept spinning. Again I heard the voice, even louder now: "Stop steering!"

This time I listened and took my hands off the steering wheel and the brakes. Within seconds, the car slowed itself down and backed gently into a shallow ditch at the side of the road. Both the car and I came out without a scratch.

In a short time a passerby pulled over after seeing me in the ditch, and drove me home. It took me awhile to contemplate what had happened; needless to say, I was in shock. After I settled down, I began to wonder about the voice that had saved my life. I couldn't stop thinking about the whole incident: the vision I had the night before, and then the voice that had helped me in my moment of terror.

I became fascinated by topics such as near-death experiences, mediumship, life after death, angels, and anything remotely connected to these themes. I read and I read and I read. This study lasted nonstop for almost four years, and during this time I went to visit a psychic who recommended that I take up meditation. I did so, and I started to have more and more clairvoyant visions.

Following two years of meditation practice, I had the experience of channeling a very powerful native spirit guide at a hands-on healing workshop. Now I work as a psychic medium, someone who holds the ability to communicate with those who have passed away. I have developed great reverence for the psychic—how could I not? My psychic connection saved my life. Thank God I thought to pray that day on the highway.

—*Lynda Flagler,*
Lindsay, Ontario, Canada

Time Travel Soldier

I saw him clear as day alongside the road. And I knew immediately who he was.

It was a comfortable August evening, with the sun just beginning to move behind the tree line but still bright. A breeze cooled the air despite the bright sun. I was passing through a construction zone with all traffic diverted to the southbound lanes of the road, but there was no delay. I was thinking how lovely the sky was with the deep blue heavens and the huge fluffy white clouds hanging like puffs of cotton.

The man was walking along the berm of the road facing traffic. He took his time, leaning a bit on the iron rod he had in his right hand. The first thing I noticed was his hat. It was dark blue, round and squat, with a small flat visor across the forehead. He wore dark blue trousers, thick and belted, with wide suspenders arching over his shoulders. His shirt was gray, short-sleeved and lighter in weight.

I couldn't see all of his boots, but I could see they were black and had rounded toes. There was a leather pouch on a strap slung over his head and draped from his left shoulder to his right hip. He had a fuzzy, dark beard that filled his face and chin.

I slowed as much as I could; there were no cars behind me but a number coming towards me. The man stopped his trek and leaned against a road sign, staring out over the highway as if he'd never seen one before. And in that moment I knew. There was only one explanation. This man was caught in a time travel snare. His "iron rod" was a long-barreled rifle with a bayonet on the end.

He was a misplaced soldier from the Civil War.

You can argue with me that it was just a scruffy man with a stick, trying to determine how much longer the road would be torn up. Or you can say that the sun was playing tricks on my vision. Maybe.

But if you had been driving east on Routes 22/119 between Blairsville and New Alexander that day, you would have seen him too. And you would be just as convinced as I am that this soldier slipped through a crack in the universe somewhere and ended up standing in front of me, watching the cars drive past as if they were the miracles that they are.

I want to believe in my soldier. I do believe in my soldier. I just hope that whoever he is, and wherever he came from, he can find his way home or make his home here, and tell everyone who would listen about the day he fell into the 21st century from 1861.

Because I saw him, clear as day, and I knew.

—*Marge Burke,*
Greensburg, Pa.

Were They Frozen in Time?

My home is on the outskirts of town in a small community that experts would most likely call a "window area." For many years, paranormal events have been occurring to me and other residents of the street.

The story of my sighting, "The Black Shadow," was published in FATE in September 2002. Kitty-corner across the street from where I saw the black shadow, the ghosts of a man and a woman were witnessed by my neighbor, Andrew F., some years before my sighting. He saw them approximately 14 times over a one-year span.

Andrew, a night owl by nature, noticed a glow in the ditch across from his house, directly beside my mobile home. Startled and curious as to its source, he stepped out onto his front porch for a better view. Still unclear as to what he was seeing, he began the long trek down his driveway. (His house sits a good distance back from the street.)

When he got halfway to the glow, he froze, unable to believe his eyes. A man and a woman stood rigid inside the glow, side by side, staring straight ahead at him as if frozen in time. Aside from their hair and clothing blowing slightly in the breeze, they were completely still. They appeared to be wearing pale blue, hospital-style gowns.

Terrified, Andrew turned and fled back to the safety of his home. "They were like holograms, projected out there," he said.

Many weeks went by, and then one night the glow reappeared. Although he was scared out of his wits, Andrew again ventured down his drive, "somehow drawn to them." This time the man was holding the woman horizontally in his arms, as if in mourning. Her eyes were closed, as if she were dead; his stared blankly ahead at my terrified neighbor. Andrew once again turned and fled back into his home.

As time went by, he tried his best to avoid the large front window that faced the ditch. He kept his sightings to himself for fear of ridicule. When the glow appeared, he would walk toward it, then retreat when he was just a few feet from the scene.

"If a car would pass by, 'they' would quickly fade from view," he said, "only to reappear when the vehicle was past."

In the final scenario he saw, the woman was lying in the ditch, as though dead. The man knelt beside her, his hand on her heart, his vacant eyes staring up unseeing into the eyes of my frightened neighbor, who once again turned and fled.

By the time he confided to me what had been playing out late at night beside my trailer, the apparitions had already ceased.

—*Suzy Driver,*
Carsonville, Mich.